*Russia,*
*America,*
*and the World*

# BOOKS BY LOUIS FISCHER

RUSSIA, AMERICA, AND THE WORLD
THE STORY OF INDONESIA
RUSSIA REVISITED
THIS IS OUR WORLD
THE LIFE AND DEATH OF STALIN
THE LIFE OF MAHATMA GANDHI
THE GOD THAT FAILED (*Co-author*)
THIRTEEN WHO FLED (*Editor*)
GANDHI AND STALIN
THE GREAT CHALLENGE
EMPIRE
A WEEK WITH GANDHI
DAWN OF VICTORY
MEN AND POLITICS (*An Autobiography*)
STALIN AND HITLER
THE WAR IN SPAIN
SOVIET JOURNEY
MACHINES AND MEN IN RUSSIA
WHY RECOGNIZE RUSSIA?
THE SOVIETS IN WORLD AFFAIRS (*2 volumes*)
OIL IMPERIALISM

# RUSSIA, AMERICA, and the WORLD

★ ★ ★ ★ ★ ★ ★ ★ ★ ★ ★

## LOUIS FISCHER

HARPER & BROTHERS   PUBLISHERS   NEW YORK

RUSSIA, AMERICA, AND THE WORLD

*To my dear friend*
*Gershon Agron*
*who is no more*

# Contents

*Russia,*
*America,*
*and the World*

# chapter 1

---

# The Cold War

THE usual assessment of the cold war as an ideological combat or a conflict of social systems distorts the shape of world affairs. Great Britain and the United States rushed to the aid of the Russian despotism the moment Hitler attacked the Soviet Union in 1941. Stalin, who exceeded Khrushchev in tyranny, received western support throughout the Second World War. The alternative of joining capitalist Nazi Germany to destroy anticapitalist communism was never considered—much less adopted—by the West.

The wartime Anglo-American partnership with the Soviets dissolved, soon after hostilities ended, into the tensions now known as the cold war. Only a very major change in the world situation could have caused such a drastic reversal. The change was, indeed, major, historic, and enduring. Stalin used the Soviet-Nazi Pact of August 23, 1939, and the war that commenced a week later to create a new Soviet empire out of East and Central European territories which he annexed outright or reduced to the status of satellites. This increased Russia's weight in Europe. With Germany and Japan defeated, damaged, and disarmed, and with England and France gravely weakened, the Soviet Union emerged from the war as the strongest nation in Eurasia, where no country or group of countries could match Muscovite military might.

One searches the record in vain for a similar expansion of

American or western power during or immediately after the war. In fact, as a result of the legitimate desire of American parents to bring their soldier boys back from overseas, reinforced by the communists' "Yanks Go Home" campaign in Europe, the United States depleted its forces abroad and weakened its armaments.

"You know, of course," President Roosevelt wrote to Prime Minister Churchill on November 18, 1944, "that after Germany's collapse I must bring American troops home as rapidly as transportation problems permit." Churchill replied the very next day that this "causes me alarm." But what caused alarm in Churchill caused joy in Stalin, for when Roosevelt told the dictator at Yalta on February 5, 1945, that he "did not believe that American troops would stay in Europe much more than two years" after the end of the war, Stalin must have decided that he could have Europe. The actual demobilization of the U.S. forces following the cessation of hostilities could be seen from Moscow only as an opportunity to extend Russia's power. Europe was psychologically distraught, economically impoverished, and politically disturbed. During 1946 and 1947 the large Italian and French Communist Parties staged numerous political strikes and in other ways made repeated bids to take over their governments. The Kremlin persisted in its efforts to gain a foothold in the Ruhr, where West Germany's rehabilitation would have to begin. In 1948 Moscow objected to the currency reform which the big three western powers nevertheless introduced in West Germany, thus laying the foundation for that country's subsequent economic recovery. The same year Stalin blockaded West Berlin in order to pinch off the city and undermine the self-confidence of West Germany. All these moves indicate that Russia aimed to achieve supremacy over all or part of Western Europe before it could recuperate from the Second World War.

Conceivably, Stalin's purpose was defensive. He wished to drive broad communist wedges into Western Europe so as to prevent a restored continent from challenging Russia's hold on Eastern and Central Europe. This is ever the way of the conqueror: he seizes one piece of territory and then needs a second to protect the first and a third to protect the second.

The United States and Western Europe disliked the extension of Soviet power into Central Europe but did nothing about it. The possibility, however, of Russia's appearance in strength in Western Europe caused alarm. It was to prevent a similar imbalance that England and America had entered both world wars.

Britain could not allow France to be crushed permanently by the Kaiser or Hitler. That would have been tantamount to German control of Europe and a menace to British national security. When the United Kingdom alone was unable to finish the job, the United States, in 1917 as in 1941, joined the fight, for the German conquest of the European continent and of the British Isles would have faced America with serious military and other problems.

After 1918 the balance of power was restored in Europe, and the United States withdrew. After the Second World War the European balance of power was again tipped sharply against the West—this time to the advantage of the Soviet Union. Only the United States could right it and keep it right. Hence America's involvement in Europe.

The United States became, in effect, the defender of three key countries of Eurasia—England, Germany, and Japan. Tsarist Russia as well as the Soviet Union had always lavished plentiful hostility on those nations. Moscow now directed it against America.

Mr. Khrushchev has on many occasions protested against the existence of American military bases in Europe and

Asia. Those bases, some on Russia's frontier, are undoubtedly an inconvenience and an irritation. One day,
when Western Europe can defend itself or when America
can render speedy and sufficient aid from its own shores, the
bases will be scrapped. For the present they maintain the
balance of power.

The history of nations is a record of balance of power
struggles. The rivalry between Egypt and Babylonia, Persia
and Greece, Greece and Rome, Spain and England, England
and Napoleon, France plus England and the Kaiser—all fit
the pattern of balance of power competitions. Coalitions and
alliances have been made, modified, and unmade to keep one
country or combination of countries from overwhelming its
competitors. Diplomatic manipulations, intrigues, dynastic
marriages, and double dealings were often the prelude to
armed conflict.

Europeans from Madrid to Moscow and Asians from
Damascus to Tokyo understand balance of power reshuffles
because their histories have been laced with them. But
Americans, wedded to isolationism and hoping to remain
aloof from world politics, expected to escape entanglement
in the essence of international affairs: the balance of power.
Yet the United States fought in two world wars to avoid
being low man on the balance of power seesaw. And today
America is one of the two chief performers in the balance of
power act called the cold war.

The current balance of power rivalry, however, has a special, unprecedented quality: it is a substitute for, not the
prelude to, a hot war. Throughout history hot wars have
been waged to alter the international balance of power in
favor of the victor. But in the age of atomic and hydrogen
bombs there would be neither advantage nor victor. The
stronger as well as the weaker side, the attacker as well as
the attacked, would suffer unimaginable destruction of lives

and property and the contamination of soil and water for
many years. No gain resulting from the war would offset this
certain loss. What would it benefit Russia if she took all of
Western Europe in a war and found ten of her cities pul-
verized?

"You underestimate the communist fanatics," a friend
has argued. "If the Kremlin could wipe out the United
States, it would not hesitate to sacrifice the hundred fifty
million Soviet citizens who might die in the holocaust."

"One hundred and fifty million dead Soviet citizens," I replied, "would leave seventy million Russians against seven
hundred million Chinese. China would then rule the Soviet
Union." Moreover, no such fanatics exist at the Soviet summit. The Muscovite leaders are sober power men; they love
themselves and their country and will not gamble with its
destruction or the decimation of their people. Nor could a
madman or drunkard in Moscow or Washington push the
button that would start the slaughter of all mankind and the
irradiation of the planet for generations. His subordinates
would not obey him. On the other hand, no general or
sergeant can start a war by firing a missile at the enemy.
American nuclear-armed rockets may not be launched, even
in case of attack, without specific orders from the President
of the United States. It is equally reassuring that the Soviet
military who observed the U-2 espionage plane overhead
deep in their territory did not shoot at it, according to
Khrushchev, until they had sent the information to him in
Moscow and received his instructions to attack it.

As invention is piled on invention, as new weapon is piled
on old, as stockpiles reach toward the rooftops, any military
adventure by either of the two giant nations becomes a pro-
hibitive risk. No one knows the exact content of the other's
arsenal; it might spell national death. The dispersal of hy-
drogen-headed missiles in submarines, old freighters zig-

zagging over the seas, and trains constantly shifting their
positions, reduces to zero the chance of a one-day or one-
hour strike that will destroy the adversary and his possibility
of retaliating.

To put the situation at its minimum: hot war cannot
enter into the calculations of any government as a conscious,
planned means of improving its balance of power status.

The fact is that, despite several serious crises since the end
of the Second World War, no test of arms has occurred between the two major cold war competitors. Whenever one of
the armed mammoths was so committed that the intervention of the second would have produced a world war, the
second abstained. This describes the position in Turkey and
Greece in 1946 and 1947, the Berlin blockade and airlift in
1948 and 1949, the Korean war from 1950 to 1953, the
Hungarian revolution in 1956, and the Lebanon-Middle
East affair in 1958. In Korea, for instance, the United States
was too deeply involved to desist. Russia therefore abstained.
In Hungary, Russia seemed too deeply involved. The United
States failed to act. The restraint displayed by both camps
suggests that the mighty instinct of self-preservation was
operating. This is the only basis we have for judging the
future.

If not a premeditated nuclear Pearl Harbor, which would
no more prevent a riposte than did Japan's original conventional one in 1941, then perhaps an accident or incident?
Perhaps, it has been said in all seriousness, a flight of geese
or starlings might show up as missiles on a radar screen.
Geese and starlings, one hears, fly every year and have
started no wars. Planes fly all year and must show up on
radar screens and some have been shot down. The Soviets
have shot down American and British planes; the West has
shot down Soviet planes. But because nobody wanted war no
war occurred. The wish must be the father of war. Suppose

the worst possible calamity took place: the captain of a jet carrying a nuclear bomb and on patrol in the air separates from his formation and heads for a Soviet city with intent to flatten it. He might be pursued and blocked or even shot down by his own command before he reached the target. He might be shot down by Soviet fighters. Suppose, however, that he succeeded in his dread design. The Soviet Union might reply by annihilating an American city of equal population. But would it, knowing that this was an accident—an isolated bombing followed by no other—order a massive retaliation and invite the same? Doubtful.

Assuredly, measures of control against accidents and against surprise attacks from the atmosphere or through space are needed. Disarmament too is an urgent necessity. Should these highly desirable goals elude mankind, however, the guarantee of safety still lies in the will of nations not to succumb to a Hiroshima multiplied a thousandfold. After some years of expending their fortune, nerves, and scientific brainpower in the endless race for elusive security, a little wisdom may be born and ultimately prevail. Fruitful negotiations might then supersede verbal figure skating at futile disarmament conferences.

But suppose two small feuding countries, say Israel and Egypt, obtained atomic or hydrogen bombs. The possession by both sides of these nation-devouring weapons would prevent their use, for the alternative would be to make Sodom and Gomorrahs of Cairo and Alexandria and of Tel Aviv, Haifa, and Jerusalem. If Israel made the bomb or acquired it from France, the United Arab Republic would likewise find a "benefactor." The resulting arms stalemate and arms race would impoverish all peoples concerned.

In the larger confrontation between the communist bloc and the West, the exclusion of hot war as an instrument of national policy puts a premium on the readjustment of the international balance of power by other—peaceful—means. The unique nuclear-age device for this adjustment is the cold war.

The cold war is the competition between the United States and the Soviet Union for the friendship, good will, diplomatic support, allegiance, and alliance of other countries. There could be no cold war if all states now allied with one or the other of the two great powers were unalterably or hopelessly allied, and if all nonaligned governments were unalterably neutral—like Switzerland, which participates in the specialized agencies of the United Nations and in UN mediation efforts but is not a member of that organization because she would then have to cast votes for or against one of the big powers. Such neutrality is unique. The international status quo, therefore, is so fluid as to leave much room for cold war courtship, pressures, and political maneuvers. For instance: Iraq was a member of the Baghdad Pact, then seceded. That alters the cold war balance. Similarly, Cuba has altered the balance of power.

The opportunities for western cold war activity within the communist orbit are few. The United States has given Poland aid, totaling several hundred million dollars, in the vain expectation that that country, held firmly in the Muscovite vise, might attenuate its ties with Russia. A number of radio "voices" from various countries seek to speak to audiences beyond the iron curtain and, now and then, western statesmen and ambassadors have appeared before Soviet TV viewers to make declarations which, though uncensored, are nevertheless tailored, at least in part, to their host's sensitivities.

This sporadic peashooting at the communist mind is the only cold war instrument available to the West in the communist orbit. Certainly, no major cold war gambits have been possible. The Russian use of tanks and troops to suppress the nation-wide uprisings in East Germany in June, 1953, and the October-November, 1956, revolt in Hungary demonstrated unmistakably that Moscow intended to thwart self-determination in its colonial possessions. China, remote, apart, opaque, remains inaccessible to the West except for occasional air forays by military photographers.

On the other hand, the whole outside world is Russia's cold war battlefield. Its back protected by the iron and bamboo curtains, communist power sallies forth into the noncommunist West and East to challenge them on their own ground. Moscow and Peking and their satellites, roaming free and far, try to make friends and influence people by trade, aid, propaganda, summit tourism, clever exploitation of chinks in noncommunist unity, and subtle use of every manifestation of noncommunist myopia.

An unabashed effort to woo France highlights one form of Moscow's cold war strategy. Throughout the protracted Algerian war the French Communist Party had condemned the policies of successive Paris cabinets. It disapproved, on September 17, 1959, of President de Gaulle's proposal, made the day before, to grant Algeria self-determination. But on October 31, 1959, Chairman Khrushchev spoke in Moscow and, as part of a cold war maneuver to loosen the entente between West Germany and France, he noted the "historically close bonds that exist between Algeria and France," and envisaged a peaceful Algerian settlement based on de Gaulle's declaration. Four days later, without a discernible blush, the central committee of the French Communist Party, "adding to and modifying" its September 17 stand, a communiqué stated, actually stood the stand on its head and echoed Comrade Khrushchev.

In the same address to the Supreme Soviet in Moscow, Khrushchev made a second remarkable statement. "We," he said, referring to Russia and France, "were allies in both world wars." "We" are the bolsheviks who, the day after they seized power in Petrograd on November 7, 1917, withdrew from the First World War and ceased being the ally of France. "We" is Stalin, who refused to fight the nazis until France had fallen to the Hitlerite despoilers. Khrushchev knew he was lying; he knew de Gaulle knew he was lying. De Gaulle knew Khrushchev knew the truth. But history to the cold warrior is a weapon. Khrushchev told the Supreme Soviet that the "interests of our two countries"—the Soviet Union and France—"clash nowhere." Peaceful regulation of the Algerian question, he added, would contribute "to the growth of France's international authority and her role as a great power." This bow to French wounded vanity and national ambition, coupled, as it was, with the usual vehement denunciations of West German "militarism" and "revanchism," constituted a Kremlin attempt to obstruct the slowly emerging unity of Europe. In effect, Khrushchev was asking France to side with Russia against Germany. He played the same tune throughout his stay in France in March, 1960. The French communists danced to his music. The success of Khrushchev's bid would substitute for NATO a Franco-Russian alliance and a German-American alliance, thus dangerously splitting Western Europe and erecting combinations ominously reminiscent of the pre-1914 period. This suggests that, while they asked others to cease waging cold war, the Soviets themselves waged it with vigor.

In the midst of the Soviet agitation for peaceful coexistence, Moscow precipitated the West Berlin crisis.

The macrocosmic cold war comes clearly into focus in the microcosm of Berlin. West Berlin is a western stronghold in a red sea. All communications between West Berlin and West Germany lie across at least one hundred miles of Soviet Germany's land, sea, and air routes. The communists are intent on capturing the island of West Berlin. Both Khrushchev and the East German leader, Walter Ulbricht, have called it a "cancer." They wish to convert it into a "free city." Ulbricht translated "free city" on October 7, 1959, when he referred in a speech to the Vatican's agreement with the Italian government which provides for free access to Vatican City and Vatican observance of Italian laws. A solution of the West Berlin issue "along these lines," he stated, "is feasible." West Berlin observance of East German laws would make the city part of the Soviet empire. This kind of dry, or cold, conquest is apparently considered compatible with peaceful coexistence.

Referring to Germany in his *Foreign Affairs* article of October, 1959, Mr. Khrushchev said, "The task before us is to do away with the aftermath of the Second World War and to conclude a peace treaty." To him, the existence of West Berlin, occupied as it is by American, British, and French troops—11,000 strong—is part of the aftermath of the Second World War. But to an even greater extent the existence of "The German Democratic Republic," occupied by more than twenty Soviet divisions, is part of the aftermath of the Second World War. If it were liquidated there would be no West Berlin problem.

West Berlin is a most unpleasant western outpost within the Soviet empire. East Germany is a broad Soviet wedge into Western Europe. Each side wishes to hold what it has and to oust its competitor. This is cold war at its most intense. Moscow insists, the West resists.

On March 5, 1960, the Soviet telegraphic agency Tass published the text of the joint communiqué signed by the Afghan government and Mr. Khrushchev after his visit to Afghanistan. The two sides, the document read, "exchanged views on the destiny of the Pathan people and agreed that a sensible way of relieving tensions and insuring peace . . . is the implementation for the solution of this problem of the principle of self-determination on the basis of the United Nations Charter." This in itself was a cold war gambit, an Afghan effort, supported by Moscow, to detach some of the Pathan people resident in Pakistan—a United States ally— and absorb them into Afghanistan. But the acceptance by Khrushchev of the principle of self-determination, first for Algerians, then for Pathans, ought to open the door for the same procedure for East Germans. A free, UN-supervised vote in East Germany, however, would result in the reunification of East and West Germany, a consummation highly unpopular in Moscow and in some western quarters as well. The cold war, accordingly, will continue to swirl around these sensitive areas.

The western troops in West Berlin had harmed nobody. There had been no incidents either with the West Berliners, who want them there as a shield against Russia, or with the Soviets. In case of war, the 11,000 troops in the West Berlin foreign garrison could have been wiped out in a flicker by the massive Russian forces in East Germany. Moscow deliberately produced the Berlin crisis.

The diplomatic attack on West Berlin was designed to strengthen the allegiance of the Poles and Czechs to Russia. The first public statement of the Soviet intention to convert free democratic West Berlin into a "free city" under their control was made by Khrushchev to Gomulka in the Kremlin on November 10, 1958. The people of Poland, East Germany, Hungary, and Czechoslovakia are not distinguished by their love of Russia. In Russia the communist regime is bolstered by Russian nationalism. In the satellites anti-Russian nationalism weakens the puppet regimes. Kremlin policy, therefore, endeavors to win sympathy for Russia by being hostile to West Germany. The Poles and Czechs are afraid of the Germans. The communists accordingly cultivate the notion that Russia is their best protector against a renewal of German expansionism. The cold war assault on West Berlin was a feature of this far-flung campaign.

Moreover, West Berlin is indeed a cancer within the East German organism. Through it, since 1949, over a million East Germans escaped to the West, thus voting against communism with their legs—the most convincing form of self-determination. Millions of other inhabitants of East Germany and of the entire Soviet empire annually make the short, easy, inexpensive trip by subway or trolley or on foot from East to West Berlin and see for themselves the contrast between eastern drabness and western sparkle achieved while consciously defending freedom. The impressions they brought back to their homes in the east were not the best communist propaganda. Nobody who has seen both West and East Berlin can believe that communism is the wave of the future.

These would have been sufficient reasons for Khrushchev to try to do by subtle means what the cruder Stalin undertook through the 1948 Berlin blockade that boomeranged. But the subtraction of West Berlin from the western world was calculated to achieve even greater side effects. Its loss would indicate to a worrying world that Moscow had, by diplomatic pressure, induced the western powers to consign into communist keeping two and a quarter million West Berliners who, time without number and right under the Soviet guns, proved their preference for western freedoms. This would hardly inspire small democracies or anybody else to trust the West and defy Moscow or Peking threats. The cohesion as well as the strength of the noncommunist world would be diminished.

If the Soviet government cannot get West Berlin, it wishes, at least, to damage the morale of West Berliners by reducing the number of protective western troops, by intensifying the subversive activities which those troops, as no other force, can exclude, and by giving the Soviet puppet regime of East Germany a recognized diplomatic status in West Berlin's life.

Moscow's designs on West Berlin fit the concept of peaceful coexistence as the Kremlin understands it. Khrushchev defined the term in a speech at Novorossisk on October 10, 1959. "Coexistence," he said, "that is the continuation of the struggle of the two social systems, but struggle with peaceful means, without war, without the interference of one state in the domestic affairs of the other state. . . . We regard this," he continued, "as an economic, political, and ideological struggle, but not a military struggle," and he told his audience what was necessary in order "to win." If winning, in the Congo for instance, requires interference in the domestic affairs of another state in contravention of a United Nations decision and the shipping of planes and trucks for military use to Lumumba as a means of drawing him closer to Russia, it is still, as Khrushchev called it, "the Leninist policy of peace and peaceful coexistence of countries with different social systems."

Lenin said something quite different. On August 23, 1915, he wrote that "it is possible for socialism to win first in a few or even in one single capitalist country. The successful proletariat of that country, having expropriated the capitalists and having organized socialist production at home, would take steps *against* the rest of the capitalist world, attracting to itself the oppressed classes of other countries, instigating in them uprisings against the capitalists, even, in case of necessity, using military force against the expropriating classes and their governments." This comes much closer than "peaceful coexistence" to a fair description of Soviet intentions and policies for many years.

Lenin also told the activists of the Moscow party organization on December 6, 1920, that "so long as socialism and capitalism endure they will not be able to live in peace: one or the other must win in the long run; the requiem will be sung either for the Soviet Republic or for world capitalism. This [period] is simply a postponement of war. The capitalists will search for pretexts to make war."

Had Lenin lived he might have grown wiser, as wise as Mr. Khrushchev, who now knows that the capitalists will not make war. Yet, according to both Lenin and Khrushchev, the two systems cannot coexist in the same world. Mr. Khrushchev feels certain that "we will bury you," and he kindly explained in America that he meant capitalism, not the capitalists.

On the one hand, Mr. Khrushchev gaily declares peaceful war, nonhot war, cold war, aimed at the destruction of capitalism—and capitalism, to him, includes everything that is not the communist dictatorship. On the other hand, he asks the capitalists to abjure the cold war and trust their impatient red undertakers. In Moscow's mouth, then, peaceful coexistence is not a road to peace but a vehicle of victory. The marked victims are reluctant to co-operate.

Khrushchev's real understanding of "peaceful coexistence" was completely clarified during his long, memorable, histrionic performance at a press conference after he torpedoed the Paris summit conference of May, 1960. Asked about the future of West Berlin, the Soviet Chairman replied that the German Democratic Republic "is a socialist republic whereas the system in West Berlin is a capitalistic one. These two systems are antagonistic and this is always fraught with conflict." He then again urged "a free city status" for West Berlin and the withdrawal of foreign troops. Then the people of West Berlin could "choose the social system under which they want to live." Time after time, in truly free elections, the people of West Berlin had chosen; they had chosen freedom. The Communist Party, free to operate in

West Berlin under a four-power treaty, received a handful of votes despite enormous sums spent on campaign propaganda. No conflict, no crisis, existed between West Berlin and the Soviet zone until Khrushchev created it. Thus coexistence, as Moscow sees it, is the prelude to conquest by cold war methods. Peace would be something quite different.

## chapter 2

# *Difficult Dialogue*

IT is difficult to carry on a conversation with a person who believes he is the epitome of virtue and you the synonym of sin. Such an exchange would be wanting in humor and fruitful results. Friendship between the two is unthinkable.

The same applies to nations.

Many problems encumber the relations between communist and noncommunist states. The problems have to be discussed, understood, then solved. The dialogue will last long. It can hardly commence if each side regards the other as eternally and inevitably wrong.

Summit tourism, notably Khrushchev's 1959 visit to America, brought some change. After seeing the United States, Khrushchev informed his people that most Americans support their government—although communist dogma requires him to say capitalist governments exploit the masses and therefore cannot enjoy popularity. He also told a Soviet audience that disarmament would not wreck America's economy—again a departure from the contention that munitions making is indispensable to U.S. prosperity. Moreover, everything the Soviet Chairman said, and much that was said to him during his American tour, appeared in the Russian press. This enabled the readers to realize, for instance, that the Kremlin version of the 1956 Hungarian revolution had not found universal acceptance. In its long first-page account of Khrushchev's dinner with American trade-union leaders in San Francisco, Moscow *Pravda* reported a statement by Walter Reuther that—translated from the Russian—"the highest stage of socialism has been achieved in Israel," where, in *Pravda*'s paraphrase, "the trade unions allegedly own sixty per cent of industry." After "own" the party newspaper inserted an exclamation point within parentheses. But that does not matter. Many Soviet citizens know how to ignore editorial punctuation.

These welcome improvements, however, do not alter the basic Kremlin principle that the Communist Party is always right because it follows the laws laid down by Marx, Engels, and Lenin; therefore the Soviet government, guided by the party, is always right. The blame for every international crisis, every unsolved problem, every threat to peace can, accordingly, rest only on the noncommunists.

The bolshevik assumption of original virtue stems from the belief that a regime born of a proletarian revolution is without sin. The Kremlin consequently throws the first stone and then more stones at all governments with less fortunate genealogies. This shapes Soviet foreign policy and propaganda. "Our desire for peace and peaceful coexistence," Nikita S. Khrushchev wrote in an article in the October, 1959, issue of *Foreign Affairs,* "is not conditioned by any time-serving or tactical considerations. It springs from the very nature of Socialist society in which there are no classes or social groups interested in profiting by war or seizing and enslaving other people's territories. The Soviet Union and the other socialist countries, thanks to their socialist system, have an unlimited home market and for this reason they have no need to pursue an expansionist policy of conquest and an effort to subordinate other countries to their influence.

"It is the people who determine the destinies of the socialist states. . . . And people of labor cannot want war."

Did the people determine the Soviet Union's destinies during the many years in which, according to Khrushchev, Stalin intimidated and even ignored the Politburo? If Soviet Russia is inherently for peace, why did she go to war against Poland and Finland? If Moscow has no need to expand, why did the Soviet government annex the eastern half of Poland and part of Rumania in 1939-1940 by agreement with Hitler? Why did Russia take over Latvia, Lithuania, and Esthonia, which Lenin had recognized as independent countries? Is it not true that the Soviet Union incorporated into its territory pieces of Germany, Finland, and Czechoslovakia? Are not Hungary, East Germany, and the other satellites "subordinate . . . to [Moscow's] influence?" How, above all, other than by Khrushchev's contempt for his foreign audience, explain his readiness to put in print statements that are contradicted by easily verifiable facts?

Not only does Khrushchev ignore these facts. Faced with them and a map that confirms them, the communist escapes into billingsgate. He shouts "Warmonger!" "Imperialist!" No reality must be allowed to cast a shadow on the immaculate record of a country which, being socialist, can do no wrong. A nonsocialist country, on the contrary, is wicked by its very nature.

Answering Khrushchev in the January, 1960, issue of *Foreign Affairs,* Mr. George F. Kennan wrote: "It will always be difficult to know how much confidence can be placed in people who appear to be deliberately deceiving either themselves or others. Is it too much to ask the Soviet leaders to drop today this Byzantine dogmatism of political thought and utterance . . . ? Scarcely anyone, surely, is deceived today by these absurd extremisms. But there are many people in

the non-Communist world to whom these recurring ev
dences of irresponsibility in the attitude toward truth are
constant source of misgiving about the prospects of an
sound and enduring coexistence between Communist an
non-Communist worlds. What can be the value of specif
understandings, these people ask, if the underlying assum
tions and beliefs are so grotesquely different? If the Sovi
leaders really think us to be as evil as they depict us to the
own people, how can they seriously believe in the possibilit
of coexisting peacefully with us?"

Many countries and governments feel self-righteous. Th
distorting historian is not a new or a uniquely Soviet ph
nomenon. But never in modern times have the rulers of
great nation won complete control over all writers and a
channels of communication and deliberately hitched ther
to current politics without regard to truth or consistency
and mindful only of the wish to prove their unfailing wi
dom and the infallibility of the governing party. The resul
is a pervasive disrespect for facts, the cynical repetition o
glaring falsehoods, a facility to alter the agreed meaning o
texts, and a disregard of treaties which obstructs the cours
of diplomatic negotiations.

One major illustration, affecting the mind of every Sovie
adult, will suffice to demonstrate the verbal jugglery prac
ticed by the Kremlin. In the summer of 1959 there appeare
in Moscow, in the Russian language, a book of 736 densel
printed pages entitled *The History of the Communist Part*
*of the Soviet Union.* The new *History* replaced *The Shor
History of the Communist Party,* published in 1938, which
as Nikita Khrushchev revealed in his secret speech on Febru
ary 25, 1956, at the Twentieth Party Congress, had beer
edited and in part written by Joseph Stalin. Khrushchev anc
Mikoyan condemned *The Short History* at the Twentieth

Party Congress. It was only a matter of time, therefore, before its successor would see the light of day.

The history of the Communist Party is required reading and study for every party member and for millions of non-party people. Its detailed version of the Soviet past, interpretation of the present, and prospectus for the future tell the Soviet citizen what to think on thousands of questions. This makes it a compulsory textbook for young and old, and when, in due course, it is translated into the tongues of the world, it also becomes the bible of international communism. In view of its crucial importance, there can be no doubt that the eleven professors and academicians who compiled the new *History* worked under the close supervision of top party leaders.

Stalin, as Khrushchev convincingly established in his secret speech, rewrote history. Khrushchev made this Stalinist operation look quite reprehensible. The new *History* is rewritten history rewritten. It never occurred to anybody to suggest that this might be equally reprehensible. The treatment accorded to Malenkov shows how simple it is.

Georgi Malenkov became a member of the party's Politburo in the 1930's. In the 1940's, as Khrushchev stated in his secret speech, Malenkov worked within the party at the right hand of Stalin. When Stalin died in 1953, Malenkov was appointed prime minister and also served as general secretary of the party. Readers will search in vain for any of these facts in the thick new *History*. The first mention of Malenkov occurs on page 654, when he is listed as a member of the "anti-party group consisting of G. M. Malenkov, L. M. Kaganovich, and V. M. Molotov." Two pages later, Malenkov and the others are purged. Who was Malenkov? The authors do not tell.

At the Nineteenth Party Congress, Malenkov delivered the

major report on the party's and the country's activities since
the previous congress. The men who wrote the new *History*
seem not to have noticed his presence. They do devote half
a page to Khrushchev's report on changes in the party's
statutes.

Perhaps the biggest lie in the new *History* is its omission
of the famous Moscow trials. During 1936, 1937, and 1938
the Moscow trials were a world-shaking event. Zinoviev,
Kamenev, Smirnov, Bukharin, Piatakov, Rykov, Radek,
Krestinsky, Rakovsky, Rosengoltz, Yagoda, Sokolnikov, and
many more topmost Soviet communists were publicly tried
and, with the exception of two or three who received prison
terms, sentenced to death and executed. The Kremlin engaged in a colossal effort to convince people at home and
abroad that these party leaders who made the Bolshevik
Revolution deserved their fate. Millions of Soviet citizens
were made to march in demonstrations and attend meetings
which demanded death for the accused revolutionaries. In
the West some called the Moscow trials "frame-ups" and
"fakes," and even those who credited the charges wondered
how so many intimate collaborators of Lenin could have
been traitors and spies.

The *Short History* calls the defendants in the first two
Moscow trials "scum of humanity" and "lackeys of the
fascists" who served "foreign bourgeois espionage agencies."
It excoriates them for plotting to assassinate Lenin, killing
Kirov in Leningrad, proposing to surrender Soviet territory
to foreign powers, engaging in sabotage, arson, explosions,
and the murder of Maxim Gorki and others. The *Short
History* ends with the events of 1937, but there is no reason
to assume that it would have been more gentle to the accused in the third trial of 1938.

The man who staged the first two trials for Stalin was
Hendrik Yagoda, head of the NKVD in the 1930's and

usually acclaimed as "the flaming sword of the revolution." In the 1938 trial he sat among the accused and was shot. His name is not once mentioned in the new *History*. Neither are the trials in which he figured as either stage director or victim.

How could this long, minute history of the Soviet communist movement, party, and government fail to make even the slightest reference to such a tremendous phenomenon as the Moscow trials? The answer is in Khrushchev's secret speech of February 25, 1956, at the Twentieth Communist Party Congress. He recalled Lenin's devastating criticism of Zinoviev and Kamenev. "But," he added, "Lenin did not pose the question of their arrest and certainly not of their shooting. Or take the example of the Trotskyites," Khrushchev continued. ". . . Many of them broke with Trotskyism and returned to the Leninist position. Was it necessary," Khrushchev protested, "to annihilate them?"

Since it was not necessary to shoot or annihilate them, the act that they were tried, sentenced, shot, and annihilated is expunged from the Soviet record. This is Socialist Realism, whose rules require a writer (and speaker) to suppress unpleasant truths and invent useful lies.

In 1918 the American, French, and British governments landed troops in North Russia. The *Short History* of 1938, when Stalin sought friendship with the United States, omits the American troops and says British and French troops intervened in North Russia. The new *History* makes it American, British, and French troops. In 1918 the Americans and Japanese intervened in the Far East. The *Short History* asserts that the Japanese intervened; it does not mention the Americans. In the new *History*, the Americans and Japanese intervened. It adds that the United States was "the arsenal" of all Russian counterrevolutionaries—which was not true.

In diplomacy, as in history, undeniable reality cannot

compete with communist dogma. On November 2, 194
after years of bloodshed and talk, Holland signed a treaty
The Hague transferring her sovereignty over the East Indi
to an independent Indonesia. A capitalist nation was givi
up an empire. Since Leninist scriptures said this could n
be, Soviet delegate Semyon K. Tsarapkin told the Unit
Nations Security Council on December 13 that "The Hag
agreements form a shameful page in the record of the Unit
Nations. . . . The shackles of colonial slavery have aga
been imposed on the Indonesian people . . . with the assi
ance of the Sukarno-Hatta clique." That the shackles
colonial slavery had actually fallen, that Holland actual
ceased to govern the Indies, was ignored because it did n
fit the communist pattern of bourgeois governments' k
havior.

More than a decade has passed; the tune remains u
changed. When almost all of Asia is free and while the Sovi
satellite, and Chinese press report that one African colo
after the other has peacefully achieved independence, t
communists denounce western imperialism with undimi
ished ferocity yet conveniently overlook their own.

Communist untruth, obviously, is a hardy growth defyi
the passage of time, dictators, and circumstances. On Septe
ber 28, 1939, Esthonia, under Soviet pressure, signed a mutu
assistance pact giving Russia military bases on the Baltic Se
On October 5 Latvia and on October 16 Lithuania sign
similar treaties with the Soviet Union. Foreign governmer
and interested groups protested. Soviet Foreign Minist
Molotov replied on October 31, 1939, that these three agre
ments "firmly stipulate the inviolability of the sovereignty
the signatory nations as well as the principle of noninterf
ence in the affairs of the other nation." He added with e
phasis: "The chatter about the sovietization of the Bal
countries is profitable only to our mutual enemies and to a

ati-Soviet provocateurs." Nevertheless, the Soviet government on July 21, 1940, annexed and sovietized the three little ountries. What price words? Words are poured like molten aetal into a mold and used as bullets to attack and paralyze ae brains of citizens and foreigners.

Reporting on the work of the party to the Nineteenth arty Congress on October 5, 1952, Georgi Malenkov said, The peoples of colonial and dependent countries are opposing their imperialist enslavers with ever-increasing determination. The struggle of the peoples of Vietnam, Burma, Malaya, the Philippines, Indonesia, the growth of nationalist opposition in India, Iran, Egypt, and other countries is evidence of the broadening scope of the nationalist-liberation aovement." It had apparently not yet dawned on him that ndia, the Philippines, Burma, Indonesia, Iran, Egypt, etc. ere independent already.

In the same report Malenkov said, "The problem of grain, ormerly regarded as the most urgent and serious problem, as been successfully solved, solved finally and irreversibly." The delegates, who included Stalin, hailed this announcement that the Soviet Union, in its thirty-fifth year, would at ast have enough bread to eat; "Stormy, prolonged applause" eads the official stenographic record. But a Communist Party ecree on March 2, 1953, declared that "the present grain roduction . . . does not meet the growing needs," and after Malenkov was dropped as prime minister, Khrushchev accused him of tampering with statistics. The supply of grain vas in fact so inadequate that under Khrushchev's energetic dministration one hundred million acres of virgin soil of aarginal quality in Kazakstan had to be plowed up to solve he grain problem again "finally and irreversibly." But at the December, 1958, plenary session of the Communist Party Central Committee, Khrushchev declared that, "as far as the roduction of grain is concerned, the country finds itself at

the same level as pre-revolutionary Russia." After all the tr
mendous expenditures of the Soviet regime on collective ar
state farms, the Soviet Union was growing no more grain tha
retarded, capitalist Russia grew under the Tsar. The ve
probable reason is that collectivization goes against the gra
of the Soviet peasant and therefore against the gra
production of the Soviet Union, but no communist dares
allude to this factor even as a suspicion.

The skill with which a communist leader can, at will, no
chalantly convert a falsehood into a vigorous assertion
truth would be worthy of admiration if it were not so d
structive of international understanding. The instances a
legion. Arguing with Vice-President Richard M. Nixon b
fore the television cameras at the American National Exhib
tion in Moscow on July 24, 1959, Khrushchev said, "On
who is for putting an end to bases on foreign lands is f
peace. One who is against is for war. We have liquidated ou
bases." He clearly implied that the United States, with mar
foreign bases, was for war. This approach is not a mere par
ing whim. During a press conference at Jakarta on Februar
29, 1960 (according to the *Pravda* of March 1) Khrushche
declared that "the Soviet Union, having liquidated the mil
tary bases which it had in foreign countries. . . ." In view
the existence of massive Soviet armed forces, with their hea
military equipment and planes, in Poland, East German
and Hungary, in view of the existence of a major Soviet nav
base at Pasha Limani Bay in the Gulf of Valona in Albani
Khrushchev's words are subject to one of only two interpret
tions: either he is propagating a lie or he regards Albani
Poland, East Germany, and Hungary as Soviet—not foreign
territory.

Western visitors to Khrushchev's office in Moscow hav
had the uncomfortable experience of attempting to contr

rt his assertion of no Soviet bases on foreign soil, but he fused to listen. His foreign ministers and ambassadors like-ise turn deaf ears on unwelcome rebuttals. And when the bject of Soviet subjugation of the satellites was mentioned the UN, Khrushchev took off his shoe and banged it on the ble.

Confronting a communist leader or diplomat the non-mmunist must take time out to analyze what he hears. "low much of this is planned propaganda?" he must ask. "low much is conscious deception?" "How much is uncon-ious and doctrinaire blindness?" Finally, "How much is uth?" For to think the Kremlin is never sincere could be a ap. It is no less dangerous for the outsider to be guided by s own preconceived notions of what communism is or what mmunists will do.

The Soviet system is bound by its doctrines to misrepre-nt. Since it is a dictatorship of the proletariat and has stroyed the exploiting classes, it must be democratic. There-re, data on the absence of democracy are taboo. Since it is cialist, it cannot be imperialist. Therefore, evidence of perialism is "counterrevolutionary propaganda." Since the orkers, peasants, and intellectuals are the people and the ople obviously favor "a people's democracy," any revolt in land, East Germany, and Hungary is the work of outside scist agents. Facts proving the contrary never get past the nsor.

It is on the basis of such an a priori principle that daily dgments are made on current events and diplomatic ac-ons.

The annals of remote and recent regimes would yield any instances of distortion, deception, and deceit. All gov-nments lie. The Eisenhower administration was in the nbarrassing position of having been caught lying about the ght of the U-2 in May, 1960. Honesty, or at least silence,

would have been a better policy. It was the gravity of d
patching the plane on the eve of the summit conference th
caused much of the trouble. The original Washington den
of the truth constituted clumsy fumbling where matur
would have been in order. But, though unpardonable, t
is not on a par with the daring rewriting of decades
Soviet history, the repeated violation of treaties, the etern
assumption of Kremlin infallibility, and the "I cannot si
stance of Moscow's leader of the day even after his predec
sor has been branded an inveterate sinner. It is trying
negotiate with a man wrapped in smug virtue.

There is "scriptural" support for communist fallibili
"The proletariat," Lenin wrote in 1916, "does not becor
holy and insured against mistakes and weaknesses only b
cause it has carried out a social revolution. But the mistak
which are possible (and the selfish interests—trying to ri
on somebody else's back) will inescapably lead it to be co
scious of this truth." Substitute "Soviet upper class" f
"proletariat" and that is the hope. It is, to be sure, a remo
hope. For to the Kremlin mind, power is a substitute f
truth, power excuses lies. In Belgrade, Edvard Kardelj, Yug
slav leader second to Tito, told me of a conversation he h
once had with Soviet Foreign Minister Vyacheslav Moloto
Kardelj explained to Molotov that the Yugoslav governme
felt bound by the requirements of national honor and trut
"I do not understand such terms," Molotov exclaime
"When you effectively control a country you are meeting a
the requirements of honor and truth."

The only way to deal with this mentality is through e
posure, composure, and a strict adherence to the truth.

## chapter 3

# The Roots of Soviet Foreign Policy

IN getting at the roots of any political problem, and of
viet foreign policy in particular, it is important to dis-
guish dogma from deed, promise from performance, and
rds from acts. A dustcloud of words makes it difficult to
termine whether the Soviets' role in world affairs is moti-
ted by world revolution or by imperialism. The Marx and
gels *Communist Manifesto* of February, 1848, declared:
The working men have no country. We cannot take from
em what they have not got. . . . National differences and
tagonism between peoples are vanishing more and more
ery day. . . . The supremacy of the proletariat will cause
em to vanish still faster. United action of the leading civi-
zed countries, at least, is one of the first conditions of the
mancipation of the proletariat." And the *Manifesto* ends
ith the ringing cry: "The proletarians have nothing to lose
ut their chains. They have a world to win. Working men of
l countries, unite!"

Like so many other statements and prophecies in the *Mani-
sto* the declaration that national differences and antagonism
etween peoples were fast disappearing was demonstrably
ntrue. Nevertheless, the goals of Marxism are therein fixed
ith firmness: internationalism and world revolution. Since
en, the doctrine of the impending and inevitable global
iumph of communism has been enunciated in a million
eeches and a mountain of pamphlets and books. Anticom-

munists, following the communist pattern of seeking to estab
lish truth by citing authority, have quoted Marx, Engel
Lenin, Trotsky, Stalin, and their lesser thought-satellites 
show that the Kremlin's central aim is a red planet.

No doubt, the Soviet leaders desire a totalitarian earth eve
as many others would welcome a world free from communis
in which democracy was triumphant. But scholastic verbiag
and wishful thinking are no proof that Soviet foreign polic
has in fact been actuated by internationalism. To draw th
conclusion from communist "holy writ" would imply a naïv
acceptance of communist propaganda at its word.

The Bible relates (Genesis 27) that in his old age, an
when he was almost blind, Isaac asked Esau, his hunter son, 
bring him fresh venison that he might eat and bless hir
Rebecca, Isaac's wife, overheard the conversation and, sur
moning her favorite son, Jacob, cooked a meat dish for hir
dressed him in kid skins—Esau was a hairy man—and tol
him to go to his father and claim the blessing. "And Isa
said unto Jacob, Come near, I pray thee, that I may feel the
my son, whether thou be my very son Esau or not. And Jaco
went near unto Isaac his father; and he felt him and said, Th
voice is Jacob's voice, but the hands are the hands of Esau

The voice is the voice of the deceiver, but the hands a
the hands of the hunter, the killer. The voice is the voice 
Karl Marx, the hands are the hands of Joseph Stalin, th
empire builder.

How, then, can one ascertain what in Soviet foreign polic
is hard essence and what verbal excrescence? The answer i
by recourse to Soviet reality inside the country. Foreig
policy, whether Russian, American, Argentine, or Japanes
always reflects domestic policies and domestic conditions.

In the late 1920's and early 1930's the Soviet Union was
deeply discontented, divided country. Stalin's one-man ty
anny had centralized power and dispersed the people's all

iance. Loyalty was to ethnic nationality, especially among the undred or more minorities, but above all to self, for the error and privations gave individual survival an urgent priority. The state was the enemy and all were its potential—millions its actual—victims. The newly collectivized peasants were disaffected, the workers underpaid and unhappy, the managers and intellectuals the objects of purges and continual official abuse. After revolver-toting NKVD men had won Stalin's "debate" with the Trotskyists the Communist Party ceased to be the source of élan, inspiration, and ideological leadership and became indistinguishable from the coercive secret police. Writers and artists, working under political instructions and censorship, had not created a new national culture or an extension of Russia's old culture. There existed, and could exist, no organic or sentimental relationship between state and people. The symbol of bolshevism was the high-walled Kremlin with its closed, guarded gates behind which the red autocrat worked in secrecy.

Stalin was too well-informed not to know that his policy of oppression and forced economic growth at the expense of consumption and freedom had lifted him to the pinnacle of a political pyramid completely hollowed out by the withdrawal of popular approval. Subsequent history proves that Stalin had no intention of moderating the terror and exploitation. Rather the contrary, they were still to mount crescendo between 1936 and 1939. Yet even a despot needs some mass backing for the smoother execution of his program, and the paranoiac in Stalin yearned for the people's plaudits though his agents organized the claque.

Stalin now switched to nationalism. He resurrected Mother Russia. At the 1943 Teheran Conference with President Roosevelt and Winston Churchill, Stalin, according to the official United States record quoted in Robert E. Sherwood's *Roosevelt and Hopkins,* said he "did not share the view of the

President that Hitler was mentally unbalanced and emph
sized that only a very able man could accomplish what Hitl
had done in solidifying the German people."

Dictators learn from one another. Watching Hitler whi
the German people into frenetic nationalism, Stalin decide
he would solidify the fragmented, atomized Soviet people b
the same means. He accordingly made nationalism the chi
ingredient of communism.

Stalin's nationalism had a strong isolationist antiwester
flavor. Two souls—the Slavophile spirit of the easterners an
the Europaphile spirit of the westerners—have long struggle
in Russia's breast. This may be explained by the fact tha
Russia spans Eurasia from west to east, by Russia's cor
version to the Eastern Orthodox Church of Byzantium i
989, by the Tatar conquests of Central Russia and th
Ukraine which cut the country off from the West from th
middle of the thirteenth to the middle of the fifteenth cer
tury, and by the mingling of a desire to imitate and equal th
industrialized, progressive West with a mystic messianism tha
smacks of Asia.

Stalin had not spent more than a few weeks in the West an
disliked what he did not know. He resented the superior cu
ture of westernized intellectuals like Trotsky and Bukharir
On August 17, 1917, he wrote, "The West exported to Russ
not so much socialism and liberation as slavery and counter
revolution." Later the West failed Russia by rejecting worl
revolution. Trotsky still believed that the salvation of th
Soviet regime lay in permanent revolution: hold out in th
Soviet citadel till the West comes to the rescue with sociali
uprisings. To which Stalin replied, "Socialism in one cour
try." Russia would be her own savior.

Astutely, Stalin tied Soviet economic modernization t
nationalism. Addressing the first Conference of Industri
Managers on February 4, 1934, he said: ". . . the history o

d Russia is one unbroken record of the beatings she suffered
r falling behind, for her backwardness. She was beaten by
ie Mongol khans. She was beaten by the Turkish beys. She
as beaten by the Swedish feudal lords. She was beaten by the
olish and Lithuanian gentry. She was beaten by the British
id French capitalists. She was beaten by the Japanese barons.
ll beat her—because of her backwardness. . . . We are fifty
 a hundred years behind the advanced countries. We must
ake good this discrepancy in ten years. Either we do it or
iey crush us."

Stalin had reason to fear that Russia might be crushed.
Vith the advent of Hitler in January, 1933, and the increas-
igly aggressive stance of the Japanese militarists, he expected
 war in which, conceivably, the country's manhood would
:fuse to die for him and his government-by-terror. Com-
iunism, the mystic idealism, had failed to conquer hearts or
:ment national unity. Stalin searched for a new, noncom-
iunist incentive.

It is possible to pinpoint the exact date in 1934 when the
oviet press first launched the word "Rodina" (Motherland).
olshevism had been envisaged by its authors as a break with
.ussia's national past. It broke up the nation. Stalin therefore
ecided to lean bolshevism on Russian history. Discarded
gures, formerly reviled, were lifted out of the dustbin and
:painted as Soviet idols. Among them were Alexander
Jevsky, a thirteenth-century feudal prince who fought the
eutonic knights; Ivan the Terrible, Peter the Great, and
:atherine the Great, the crowned parents of Russian expan-
ionism; General Alexander Suvorov, who led Russian armies
gainst revolutions in Europe; and Prince Kutuzov, who
rappled with Napoleon on the plains of Russia.

Stalin nourished nationalism by every possible means:
Russians had invented the electric bulb, wireless, the air-
lane, and what not; Russian mathematics, Russian science

excelled; Soviet literature was best because it was socialis
Foreign communists were told that defense of the Sovie
Union was the highest form of internationalism. Stalin said i
a speech on August 1, 1927: "An internationalist is one wh
unconditionally, unwaveringly, without conditions is ready t
defend the Soviet Union, for the Soviet Union is the base c
the world revolutionary movement, and it is impossible t
protect and to advance that revolutionary movement withou
protecting the Soviet Union."

To "protect" the Soviet Union, foreign communist partie
undermined western resistance to Hitler until Russia wa
attacked in 1941; defended the Soviet-Nazi Pact which the
had previously called impossible; staged revolts which wer
doomed before they began; defended all of Stalin's brutalitie
purges, and lies until Khrushchev condemned them in hi
1956 secret speech; and justified Soviet suppression of th
Hungarian revolution. But I know of no case in which th
Soviet government made a measurable sacrifice in the intere∫
of the world revolutionary movement or of a foreign com
munist party.

Thus Stalin went beyond fathering nationalism inside th
Soviet Union. He placed the entire world communist move
ment at the service of Soviet national interests to the detr
ment of international communism. Moscow's principle wa
"Russia Ueber Alles."

The best food for jingo nationalism is foreign territory, an
the acquisition of foreign territory is imperialism. Imperial
ism, Lenin notwithstanding, is not the last stage of capitalism
it is the first, middle, and last stage of aggressive nationalism

The present era of Soviet imperialism began with th
annexation of half of Poland, all of the Baltic countries, an
parts of Finland and Rumania by force and by Hitler's leave
No internationalist, socialist, or Marxist would have seize
independent lands in this fashion. But Stalin was a nationalist

When Churchill reminded Stalin at the Teheran Conference that the bolsheviks had come to power in 1917 proclaiming "No annexations, no indemnities," Stalin replied, "I told you that I am becoming a conservative." On occasion Stalin did tell the truth. He had become a conservative, a conservative, anti-Marxist imperialist—like Churchill. No internationalist would have telegraphed to Ribbentrop in December, 1939, that "the friendship of the peoples of Germany and the Soviet Union, cemented in blood, has every reason to be lasting and firm." (Presumably the blood was Polish and it had been shed by Hitler and Stalin.) Nor would an internationalist have incorporated parts of East Prussia into the Soviet Union; he would have given them to communist East Germany.

The Soviet empire, embracing foreign territories annexed outright or dominated as satellites, stems solely from the military conquests of the Soviet armies. One communist country, Yugoslavia, not fully occupied by the Russian forces, could liberate itself and become independent. Another communist country, China, is too big and strong to be subjugated by Russia. The Soviet empire is thus a triumph of Soviet national power, not of the communist world revolution. In fact, Soviet colonialism documents the failure of the world revolution and the victory of nationalism.

The Soviet Union fought the Second World War under the banner of nationalism. The war was and is officially "The Great Fatherland War." Pan-Slav propaganda abounded. Communism was almost never mentioned.

A Georgian by birth, Stalin nevertheless functioned as a Great Russian nationalist. He called himself "a Russian bolshevik," though to a true bolshevik "bolshevik" would have sufficed. In his report to the Sixteenth Party Congress on June 27, 1930, Stalin proclaimed that the Great Russians, who constituted just over half the population of the Soviet Union, were culturally superior to the Ukrainians and White Rus-

sians and far superior to his fellow Georgians and to Ar
menians, Kirghizes, Turkomans, etc. After the war Stalin
praised the Russian people, as distinct from other national
ities, for their "clear intelligence, stable character, and pa
tience." At a banquet of Red Army officers on May 24, 1945
a fortnight after Germany's surrender, Stalin, reminiscing
about the difficult period in the first years of the war, declared
that "the Russian people" had stood by him in the darkest
hour. "Thank you, Russian people, for your trust!" he ex
claimed.

Outside the Soviet Union, the words "Russian" and
"Soviet" are often used interchangeably. But in the U.S.S.R.
the emphasis on "Russian" has a special significance. To say
"Russian" for "Soviet" is to make a racist, narrow-national
istic distinction in favor of the Great Russians of Central
Russia and Siberia and against all the many other national
ities of the country. Stalin did this deliberately. He knew he
could not modernize the Soviet Union or fight a successful
war without the good will, patriotism, and ardor of the Great
Russians, who were indeed the most advanced segment of the
population technologically and culturally, and of the Ukraini
ans, who rank next to them in numbers and ability. Stalin
meant to purchase their eager collaboration with concessions
to their nationalism as well as with material benefits to their
upper class. For the Great Russians he annexed territories
which the tsars had stolen and Lenin had liberated. For the
Ukrainians he brought into the Soviet Union all the Ukrai
nian-inhabited domains of Eastern Europe, including a slice
of Czechoslovakia, and then tried to convince them that their
forefathers who had united the Ukraine with Russia more
than three centuries ago were the truest patriots.

The Kremlin has de-Stalinized and re-Stalinized; it canno
discard the essence of Stalinism. Khrushchev stands on Stalin's
shoulders. The four pillars of today's Soviet system are stil

Stalin-made: industrialization, collectivization, one-party dictatorship, and empire.

The most potent public sentiment in the Soviet Union today is patriotism. No government is more attentive to matters of national grandeur, power, pride, and prestige than the Soviets. Nationalism has become the cohesive element of the state and the ruling ideology—though emotion would be a better word. *Pravda,* for instance, replied with an uncompromising no to the suggestion of Mr. Brundage, chairman of the 1960 Olympics committee, and vice-chairman Lord Exeter that the word "national" be eliminated from the Olympics charter so as to reduce national rivalry and let each participant compete as an individual.

When Khrushchev was in London with Bulganin in 1956, the British leaders broached the subject of German reunification. Khrushchev's reply, repeated to me by one of the Englishmen, was: "If I came back to Moscow and reported that I had agreed to reunification, people would say, 'It's a pity Stalin died.' "

This would suggest that in Khrushchev's opinion his role as Stalin's heir would be jeopardized by the surrender of East Germany. He may be right. And he perhaps undertook the cold war gambit against West Berlin in order to reinforce the Soviet grip on the undemocratic "people's" republic of Germany and thus prevent any untoward event there from undermining his strength at home. For empire and personal eminence are closely interlinked. In December, 1956, shortly after Russia almost lost Poland and Hungary, Khrushchev almost lost his number one position.

The assault on Khrushchev at the December, 1956, plenum of the Soviet Communist Party's Central Committee was a battle in the war for supremacy between Georgi M. Malenkov, the clearest-eyed statesman in the Kremlin, and Nikita S. Khrushchev, conscious of the talents he subsequently displayed. When Stalin died in March, 1953, Malenkov occupied the two summit posts: he was prime minister and general secretary of the party. A few days later, to diminish this concentration of power, Khrushchev became temporary party secretary. Malenkov suffered a further depletion of strength through the execution, on July 10, 1953, of his ally, Beria, the secret police chief. Malenkov lost another battle when the party confirmed Khrushchev as party secretary on September 13, 1953. Khrushchev finally won the war on February 8, 1955, the day Malenkov "resigned" as prime minister and became minister of power stations.

However, the brief revolt in Poznan, Poland, in June, 1956, and the anti-Soviet upsurges in Poland and Hungary later that year, which seemed to threaten the empire, supplied Khrushchev's numerous enemies—for *he* had acquired too much power—with ammunition against him, and they combined, each with his own motive, to take economic affairs out of his hands and place them under Mikhail G. Pervukhin, a member of the party Presidium and supporter of Malenkov. The Malenkov-Pervukhin-Saburov group apparently reflected the view of the new generation of Soviet industrial managers who urged more production for consumption rather than the continued emphasis on heavy industry at the expense of living standards. Malenkov was also a "liberal" in foreign policy. The continuing communist tirades against Malenkov and Beria accuse them of offending against "proletarian internationalism" and, since "the dictatorship of the proletariat" means dictatorship by one or two or three leaders, since dictatorship is democracy, one is entitled, by the same method of inversion, to interpret "proletarian internationalism" to mean Soviet imperialism. The charge may indeed be true. Foreign experts on Soviet questions have written that Beria in 1953 suggested the abandonment of East Germany in order to

lessen tension with the West, thereby enabling Russia to reduce her armaments and increase the supply of consumers'
goods in accordance with the wishes of the Malenkov man-
agerial group and, needless to say, of the people.

Khrushchev's power, shaken in December, 1956, was re-
established by clever maneuvering at the February, 1957,
party plenum. The next month he launched his program of
economic decentralization which would disperse the control
theretofore exercised by the Moscow managers who resented
the day-to-day intervention by political party bosses—notably
Khrushchev—in the complicated task of running modern
industry. By June, 1957, Khrushchev purged Malenkov, Molotov, Kaganovich, and Foreign Minister Shepilov from the
cabinet and party leadership and relegated them to minor
posts to be followed some months later by Prime Minister
Bulganin.

Khrushchev's victory was in considerable measure due to
the support given him by Marshal Georgi Zhukov, the popular wartime hero and minister of defense. Khrushchev was
in league with the army, which wanted arms, against the
managers, who would have given it less. But he must have
reasoned that if Zhukov had power enough to help him triumph over his enemies he was too powerful for comfort.
Besides, now that the enemies had been dismissed, Khrushchev no longer needed Zhukov, who, accordingly, disappeared into a void. This is an old Stalinist tactic. Stalin
defeated Trotsky with the aid of Zinoviev and Kamenev, then
defeated Zinoviev and Kamenev with the aid of Rykov,
Tomsky, and Bukharin, then purged them. Zhukov made
Khrushchev's task easy by going off to hunt wild goats with
Tito in the Yugoslav mountains and from there traveling even
farther afield to Albania. On his return to the Moscow airfield
he was met by one officer, who told him he had instructions to

escort him to his home, which of course had been isolated. In such circumstances, a man is only a man and physical resistance is folly.

Having achieved a position of supremacy but not of omnipotence, Khrushchev maneuvered to keep his power and enhance it. Already the secretary of the party—the office carrying the greatest weight in the Soviet Union—he also made himself chairman of the Council of Ministers, or prime minister. This enabled him to function as the single Soviet representative in travels to foreign countries instead of sharing the limelight in trips abroad or to summit conferences with a Bulganin or other figure of less influence. The success of his visit to America, for instance, was booked by the Soviet press to him alone and produced a rather clear case of the old and reviled cult-of-personality disease.

As the head of the government, moreover, Khrushchev enjoyed some automatic prestige. Many Soviet citizens, even if anticommunist, are proud of their country's achievements at home and its power abroad. A country must have a government, and citizens normally accord the government's chief their homage.

Among Soviet leaders from Lenin to the present, Khrushchev is unique in seeking both legitimacy and popularity to bolster his political power. Conscious of a number of trends in Soviet life, Khrushchev has endeavored to favor as many of them as he can. Thus he seems to feel that he could not remain the Kremlin's first minister if he presided at the liquidation of the Soviet empire. In his determination to maintain and perhaps reinforce it he has considerable support from the political leadership, the army, the people, and from the communists in the satellites who would lose their jobs if the empire disappeared.

There are, however, contrary, or at least different, Soviet pressures coming from the industrial managers whose outstanding representative in the Kremlin was Georgi Malenkov. The managers are undoubtedly happy to make the sputniks, luniks, missiles, and jets which so impress the outside world. In any case, they manufacture what they are told. But if they have anything in common with American managers—and logically, and according to some evidence, they do by virtue of their similar function as producers—they would like to pour out more and more goods for a human market that could absorb them.

Khrushchev has been trying to mollify the industrial managers. He brings them into high party councils, including sessions of the supreme Central Committee, of which they are not members. The supply of commodities for daily consumption has been increased. Khrushchev's most difficult internal task is perhaps to prevent a split between the upper class of technocrats and the high-ranking bureaucrats of the party. The latter sometimes interfere too much in the work of the former; the former include military officers.

What has happened is a concealed yet undeniable differentiation in the Soviet upper class. Party, army, and technocracy are endeavoring to keep or enlarge their share of power. At present the party is superior. It is the capitalist segment of the upper class, for it controls though it does not own—there is no ownership—the means of production. The army and the technocracy are the functional segments of the upper class. They use the means of production. Control by politicians is resented by the specialists who perform indispensable services. The military and managers are challenging the Communist Party and its obsolete liturgy and texts. The age of science and technology is trying to elbow the age of ideology off the Soviet stage.

The party-army-technocracy rivalry suggests a certain parallel with English history in 1215 when the barons at Runnymede extracted the Magna Carta from King John. The

barons were probably no better democrats than the members
of the Soviet upper class. But they wanted more rights for
themselves and more limited prerogatives for the sovereign.
That began a long process of enfranchising the disfranchised
which resulted in today's democratic Britain. It took about
seven hundred years. It started where the demand for democracy always starts—at the top, and filtered downward. It
has commenced, almost imperceptibly, in Russia. It may last
long. Or modern tempos may accelerate change.

Already the requirements of the Soviet upper class for that
peace of mind and personal security indispensable to efficient
work has been responsible, to an important degree, for the
cessation of political arrests and executions after Stalin's
death. Civil rights, however, are still nonexistent. The citizen
is an instrument, not the sovereign. The state is sovereign,
and Khrushchev and a few of his colleagues are the state.

This is relevant to foreign policy and imperialism. Alexander Herzen (1812-1870), a Russian writer and publicist and
forerunner of the bolsheviks, wrote: "You cannot begin an
era of freedom in your homeland if you put a rope around the
neck of your neighbor." He said this apropos of Poland; it
could be said of Poland, Hungary, and the other Soviet satellites today. Soviet imperialism retards the progress toward
more liberties and therefore toward more groceries. This is
not without some relevance even for a country like England,
whose history and traditions are so vastly different from
Russia's. Great Britain was quite democratic before 1945. But
for millions the content of British democracy was enriched by
the introduction of free medical care for all, expanded education, full employment, and the leveling up of social classes
that coincided with withdrawal from empire in Asia.

Writing on July 15, 1903, Lenin approvingly quoted Marx
as follows: "So long as we [Germans] help to oppress Poland,
so long as we bind a part of Poland to Germany—we ourselves

remain bound to Russia and Russian policy, we ourselves cannot make a radical break at home with patriarchal-feudal absolutism. The establishment of a democratic Poland is the primary requisite of a democratic Germany." Substitute Russia for Germany and Marx's statement applies to current world affairs: the establishment of a democratic Poland is a primary requisite of the establishment of a democratic Soviet Union.

"A nation that oppresses foreign peoples cannot be free itself," Marx wrote on another occasion. Lenin quoted this on December 12, 1914. Soviet imperialism prolongs the life of the Soviet dictatorship.

The Soviet Union has reached the point in its social development where the dictatorship no longer fears the people, who are either docile enough or patriotic enough or, in the case of the upper and middle classes, materially prosperous enough to accept the government. Moscow, accordingly, can dispense with terror as the chief instrument of administration. It does not have to create foreign or domestic enemies in order to justify the use of draconic measures. It does not require tensions outside to justify tensions inside; the inside tensions are diminuendo. Except for purposes of cold war, it need not resort to the creation of international crises.

Berlin is an instance of a cold war crisis artificially precipitated to strengthen Russia's hold on Poland, East Germany, and Czechoslovakia and, too, to strike a sympathetic chord among the Soviet population which suffered so grievously at the hands of Germany during the Second World War. But for the satellites, Moscow would reduce the intensity of its cold war activities. But for the satellites—and China.

"Only a free Russia that is under no necessity to oppress the Poles, Finns, Germans, Armenians, and other small nationalities or constantly to incite France against Germany," Lenin wrote in 1895, "will relieve contemporary Europe of its military burdens, weaken the reactionary elements in Europe, and strengthen the European working class."

In the Kremlin's oppression of Poles and other small nationalities and in Khrushchev's constant incitement of France against Germany, Lenin would have recognized an extension of tsarist foreign policy.

Russia's current control of foreign nations places heavy military burdens not only on contemporary Europe and America but on the Soviet population as well. The price of the Soviet Union's active participation in the cold war is, if one includes the cost of armaments, aid to the satellites and China, and assistance to Asian and African countries, an enormous one which palpably lowers Soviet living standards.

Khrushchev, returning through Siberia after his trips to the United States and China, addressed several large meetings en route. At Bratsk, where a giant hydroelectric power station was under construction, he told the assembled workers, according to Moscow *Pravda* of October 10, 1959, that there would be no world war because the Soviets had put their emblem on the moon and because Americans knew any spot on their map could be attained by Soviet missiles. Russia was building communism, he declared; they were building communism.

What followed is translated verbatim from *Pravda:* "What else would you want to hear from me?" Khrushchev asked.

"A Voice: 'When will the prices of manufactured goods be reduced?' "

One can almost hear Mr. Khrushchev drop with a thump from the moon and America to the hard reality of the Soviet worker's daily life. "N. S. Khrushchev: 'The reduction of prices of some manufactured goods has been carried out in our country systematically, and this you well know. You also know well that the prices of goods can be lowered only when more of those goods are produced and when the productivity of labor rises up and up and the cost of production goes down.

" 'Am I right? (Exclamations: 'Right.' Applause.)

" 'I was myself a worker for a long time and I know very well what work is. Of course it is possible without further ado to lower the prices of goods, but then where would we get the means for the further development of the national economy? Do you think God will send us new plants, factories, electric stations? If, without taking account of real possibilities, we lower the prices of goods, or if, without considering anything, we raise wages, will that facilitate the development of our national economy? Of course not. We would then consume our accumulated savings, we would not receive new savings, and could not build such great electric stations like yours and others.' "

At another meeting during the same Siberian trip, Khrushchev said, "Perhaps there are some among you who are wearing [felt or bast] boots and would like a good pair of shoes."

"There are such, there are such," members of his audience interrupted.

"The same goes for the Soviet state," Khrushchev retorted.

Forty-two years after the launching of the Bolshevik Revolution, after sufferings, mental torments, physical hardships and deaths—thirty million in the Second World War—unprecedented in the history of any one nation, Khrushchev was still asking the Soviet people to make further sacrifices to the "great god state," that is, to the dictatorship.

Khrushchev travels much to villages and towns. In one place he stopped and asked a woman about living conditions. Conditions were fine, she told him, according to his own account. "As soon as it became known that you were coming here," she said, "the shops filled with shoes, textiles, fish, milk, and many other commodities. Come oftener, Comrade Khrushchev."

The Soviet public is also informing the Kremlin—by the direct action of not buying—that the quality of consumers' goods is unsatisfactory. All statistics of Soviet production of manufactured foods and commodities, of housing and transportation facilities, must be reduced by a coefficient of bad quality. Thus, if, to take an arbitrary figure, the country has an output of 300 million pairs of shoes which wear out in six months instead of eighteen months, the actual output is only 100 million pairs, and a great deal of labor, machinery, and administrative overhead has been wasted. One of the difficulties in assessing the Soviet national economy is that the Kremlin does not keep books on real costs in terms of lives, health, nerves, materials, rubles, and hours lost.

The Soviet people can now see the results, in the shape of new cities, industries, and farms, of their almost inhuman labors for nearly half a century to build up their country. Yet compared to the energy expended the rise in living standards has been woefully low. And by absolute standards it is much lower than that of most Western European countries, of the prewar British dominions, and of the United States. The reason is that in no noncommunist country is such a large percentage of economic effort devoted to armaments, the financing of the bureaucratic state, subsidies to satellites, and foreign aid at the expense of the goods and services for which the population continues to clamor.

"Although we have no surplus capital," Chairman Khrushchev told the parliament of India on February 11, 1960, "we are rendering ever-increasing assistance to states needing such aid." If a nation without surplus capital makes long-term (mostly twelve-year) loans totaling several billion dollars at uncommercially low interest rates for cold war purposes and, in addition, builds stadiums, hotels, and hospitals as gifts to underdeveloped countries for propaganda purposes, the daily living conditions of its own people suffer. At best such aid represents delayed consumption for the Soviet masses, whose entire history has been one of delayed consumption. More probably it constitutes an absolute loss to their welfare. The postponement of pie in the interest of state power has been the outstanding feature of Soviet life these forty-three weary years. That the dawn of material well-being in the shape of higher wages and lower prices should be put off, as Khrushchev said at Bratsk, in order to build this power station and others is no comfort to men and women who are told hourly that they will soon catch up with America. Among the "other" power stations should be included the High Dam in Egypt and, by translation, the steel mill in India and scores of plants which Russia is erecting in the Soviet empire and beyond.

One would like to view this as a human problem. This is not how the Soviet leaders see it. The question is whether it has become a political problem. At the least, the Kremlin knows from Khrushchev's contacts with the people and from other sources how impatient they are to enjoy more of the fruits of their labor. This may not be decisive. Does the discontent of the nation with living conditions adversely affect output in factories and on farms? Does that spoil the political mood of the technocrats and managers? How does it affect the growth of population? (Because of goods shortages and bad housing, Soviet families seem to be limiting the number of births. Though the Soviet Union—with 208 million inhabitants in 1959, on an area the size of North America—is seriously underpopulated, the government in 1955 was forced to relegalize abortions, which had been made illegal in 1936.) These are the realistic considerations which might—not today or tomorrow—induce second thoughts in the Kremlin about the wisdom of empire and of its present intensive cold war campaign. Some day an "Attlee" will emerge in Moscow who would gladly preside over the liquidation of the empire and see it as opening an opportunity to improve the lot of the underprivileged and thereby launch the kind of new social revolution which Great Britain has witnessed, under Labour and Conservative governments, since 1945. One thing is clear: in an age when nearly all of Asia has thrown off the yoke of imperialism and much of Africa is hastily doing so, it seems incongruous for European countries to be subject to the wishes of a "motherland" their people never chose.

In the present unfortunate world situation, the first political obligation of a government is national defense. The loss of empire, however, and the relaxation of Russia's endeavors to enhance her power and influence at the expense of other nations, would not reduce her strength or security. The Soviet press and leaders no longer mention "the capitalist encirclement" of Russia. It is nonexistent. There is no indication or evidence that the Soviet authorities are afraid of Germany or the United States or both of them and the nations associated with them. In the summer of 1959 Khrushchev told a group of German social democratic newspaper editors that eight hydrogen bombs could wipe out West Germany—and it is not speculation that the Soviets possess many times eight. Khrushchev warned on November 10, 1958, that no matter how hard the German militarists tried "they cannot alter the power relationships in their favor, and they also cannot forget the geographic position of West Germany which, with war techniques as they are now, could not survive one day of modern war." In Paris, on March 23, 1960, Khrushchev told a press conference that for Germany "to make war on the Soviet Union is the equivalent of suicide." There can be no question that he is right.

"I am emphasizing once more," Khrushchev said to the Supreme Soviet in Moscow on January 14, 1960, "that we already have so many nuclear weapons, both atomic and hydrogen, and the necessary rockets for sending these weapons to the territory of a potential aggressor, that should any madman launch an attack on our state or on other socialist states we would be able literally to wipe the country or countries which attack us off the face of the earth." He then mentioned a "fantastic weapon" which "is being developed" in the Soviet Union, and raised the question whether some capitalist nation "will draw level with us" and "attack us first in order to make use of the unexpectedness of attack. . . . No," he declared, "contemporary means of waging war do not give any country such advantages."

Khrushchev's complete confidence in the power of the Soviet Union to defend itself has been voiced repeatedly by him and other Kremlin spokesmen, and if anyone doubts their words he may judge by their actions, which reflect no fear. When the Soviet government was afraid of Japan it sold the Chinese Eastern Railway in 1935 to the Japanese puppet in Manchuria. When Stalin was afraid of Hitler from 1939 to 1941 he groveled before the nazi. The present Moscow mood is just the opposite and, given their enormous military capacity, fear would indeed be folly.

Fear is a poor counselor in international politics. Fear fathers distrust. With Soviet fears at a minimum and internal pressures for a better life increasing, the outlook for a ban on nuclear tests, for disarmament, and for political settlements should improve. One of the major remaining obstacles is noncommunist suspicions of Russia, which are nurtured by her secretiveness and especially by her competitiveness. Though the Soviet Union has abolished competitive private enterprise, it fosters "socialist" competition at home between factories, farms, ministries, regions, and so forth with a view to introducing an unpaid incentive to increase production—a peculiar, communist form of exploitation. In fact, at home and abroad, the Soviet Union is the most competitive country in the world. It proclaims its ambition to overtake and surpass America in per capita output of milk, meat, and strawberries, and for the sake of the individual one hopes it will. Its high officials come to the United States and other lands and with the gaucherie of the nouveaux riches shout loudly, on the day of arrival, "By us everything is better." Would that it were. Soviet sportsmen strive hard to win in international matches, as they of course should, and when they lose the matter is subjected to Marxist analysis in the newspapers. Happily they have won at the Rome Olympics and on other occasions. Perhaps that will satisfy their craving to be first and highest and still their hunger for supremacy in new fields of political power. Russian leaders have ever been painfully aware of their backwardness and pathologically eager to disprove it. In conferring the title of emperor on Tsar Peter the Great, Chancellor Count Golovin said, "By thy untiring labors and by thy sole leadership, we have stepped forth from the darkness of insignificance and ignorance on the road of glory and have joined in equality with the civilized states of Europe." It sounds exactly like a statement Zhdanov or Malenkov might have made to "the Great Stalin."

Soviet successes in science and economics may, in time, diminish the mad competitive urge to national self-assertion. This would be a long step in the direction of weakened world tensions. Every opportunity should be granted Russia to "join in equality" with the civilized states of the world. A policy of relegating her to second place is impossible, unnecessary, and harmful. A large segment of international politics has nothing in common with legal texts and official agreements. It is psychology and needs delicate treatment by sensitive persons.

Statesmanship nowadays has become salesmanship, and Nikita S. Khrushchev deserves to be recognized as the greatest traveling salesman of the age. In this respect he has already overtaken and surpassed America, the land of the salesman. He out-Madison-Avenues Madison Avenue. The demagogue has eclipsed the idealogue and threatens the democrat. Shrill advertising slogans drown out the still small voice of diplomacy. Propaganda is trumps. The target for tonight is tomorrow's headline. But big complicated problems involving the fate of mankind are not soluble in shouts before the microphone. Political wrestling matches on television do not conduce to a calm climate in which serious leaders can come to grips with the troubles that torment the earth's inhabitants. It is better not to run races with Khrushchev in the gambling-casino-marketplace atmosphere he creates. The tool of the statesman is patient, optimistic, self-confident toil in pursuit of basic solutions.

A government's acts are not to be judged by, and therefore should not be directed to, their immediate propaganda impact or their immediate political result. What counts are the living conditions, happiness, and creative development of the country's and other countries' people. If the Soviet government addressed itself more to the welfare of its subjects and the peace of the world it would abandon the imperialism which emerged when it switched to aggressive nationalism and substitute friendly coexistence for angry competitive coexistence. If the Soviet government wanted disarmament it would not propose total global disarmament in four years which it knows nobody, not even the neutrals who have backed the proposal, can accept. If Khrushchev really desired a summit conference for negotiation he would not dictate the results of the talks before the meeting was opened.

From all appearances, the makers of Soviet foreign policy are not yet ready for "peace and friendship." But Russia has seen many changes and will see more.

## chapter 4

# The Russian Bear and the Chinese Tiger

NATIONS behave like nations. This sounds obvious or trite but it is the essence of international politics. Nations behave like nations irrespective of their ideologies or social and political systems. Democratic nations have fought wars against democratic nations, Christian nations have fought Christian nations, Moslem nations have been the enemies of Moslem nations, totalitarian nations have fought totalitarian nations (nazi Germany versus communist Russia), democracies have supported communist dictatorships (United States aid to the Soviet Union during the war and to Yugoslavia since the war), and imperial Russia has been in serious conflict with nationalistic Yugoslavia though both call themselves communist.

It is in this perspective that the relations between the Soviet government and Red China should be examined. Theoretically at least, China can be a problem to Russia. In fact, the problems and puzzles which Soviet Russia has posed to the world since the 1917 Bolshevik Revolution will perhaps seem minor when communist China achieves her potential of economic and military power. Historians may then decide that the biggest phenomenon in the second half of the twentieth century was the rise of Red China.

The only Chinese types we used to recognize were laundrymen, comic pigtailed figures shuffling across the vaudeville stage, and soldiers straggling into battle with umbrellas over their heads when it rained. The Mao regime has shown that the comic figures are those whose vision was so limited. Chinese have stamina, industry, manual skill, mental agility, trading ability, financial acumen, diplomatic finesse, organizing talent, and great capabilities as warriors. Red China's population already numbers 650 million and is multiplying at the rate of at least 15 million a year. By 1980—it won't be long now—China should have a billion inhabitants. China, to be sure, is much poorer than Russia in known natural resources and, with three times the population of the Soviet Union, has about half as much arable land. Nevertheless, a billion-headed nation—one third of the human race—united and harnessed to a power-minded political machine intent on raising production and expanding its fighting strength is something new and something to be reckoned with.

Because the enormous reality of Chinese communism emerged so suddenly and menacingly, many meet it behind a shield of unreality: they exclude it, refuse to recognize that it is there, hope for its collapse, and construct imaginary combinations against it. The Eisenhower administration dreamed of "unleashing" Chiang Kai-shek—sending forth the sparrow to slay the tiger.

China, one is aware, has not solved her food problem. Yet what counts in a dictatorship is not individual welfare but state power and its aggressive propulsion. Here China has made enough gains to alter the shape of world affairs and to foreshadow further increases in her international weight. China is astir.

"China, there lies a sleeping giant," Napoleon is reported to have said. "Let him sleep, for when he awakes he will shake the world." This specter may explain why, after 1898, the disturbed statesmen proceeded to hack the giant into British,

Russian, Japanese, German, and French pieces called "spheres of influence." Only the United States, through Secretary of State John Hay's open-door policy of 1900, held up an ineffective minatory finger.

Russia's share embraced Outer Mongolia and Manchuria. She lost part of Manchuria after her defeat by Japan in 1905; weakness following the Bolshevik Revolution forced a complete withdrawal from foreign territories. But in the 1920's the new Russia resumed the Tsar's old place in Outer Mongolia and contested Japan's imperial monopoly in Manchuria. The 1945 military collapse of Japan permitted Moscow to retake Manchuria entire and make a satellite of North Korea.

These acquisitions and the appetite for more would logically have prejudiced Stalin against any regime, communist or not, that might unite China. He had always harnessed outside communist parties to Soviet foreign policy, but there is no evidence that he ever favored communist revolution in a country so big or so far from Russia's frontiers as to raise the possibility of its existence independently of Moscow's will. Stalin feared what later became known as Titoism—a communist regime free from Muscovite hegemony.

In 1926 Trotsky, still a factor in Soviet politics, urged nudging China toward communism. Stalin demurred and threw his support to Chiang Kai-shek. Subsequently Chiang began beheading communists and Stalin, for a time, disavowed his protégé. But Mao Tse-tung never became Stalin's favored Chinese. Stalin once actually told a small secret conference that he did not want a communist China.

It is rare to have classified information about top-level communist deliberations. But Tito's defection made disclosure possible. On February 10, 1948, a meeting took place in Stalin's office at which he, Molotov, Zhdanov, Suslov, and Zorin represented Russia; Dimitrov, Kolarov, and Kostov spoke for Bulgaria; and Kardelj, Djilas, and Bakariĉ for Yugoslavia. Four months later Tito broke out of the Soviet orbit and his biography, really an autobiography dictated to Vladimir Dedijer, edited by Tito, and published in New York and elsewhere in 1953 under the title *Tito,* gives a verbatim report of the proceedings based on the written reports of the Yugoslavs present. "It is true," Stalin said at the conference, "we have also made mistakes. For instance, after the war we invited the Chinese comrades to come to Moscow and we discussed the situation in China. We told them bluntly that we considered the development of the uprising in China had no prospect, and that the Chinese comrades should seek a *modus vivendi* with Chiang Kai-shek, that they should join the Chiang Kai-shek government and dissolve their army. The Chinese comrades agreed here with the view of the Soviet comrades, but went back to China and acted quite otherwise. They mustered their forces, organized their armies, and now, as we see, they are beating the Chiang Kai-shek army."

Stalin's acts confirm his words. Russia's Red Army transported Chinese communist regiments into Manchuria in 1945 to compete with Chiang Kai-shek units brought there in American ships. The Chinese communists enjoyed an advantage over Chiang because the Russian occupation troops armed and supported them. With Mao's help, Stalin meant to hold Manchuria as his fief and prevent it from fulfilling its natural function as the industrial base of a new, developed China. To this end the Soviet government denuded Manchuria of machines, railway equipment, and mineral stockpiles and then blew up dams and power stations.

Stalin wanted a weak Chiang Kai-shek China further weakened by communist subversion throughout the country and by Russian control of Manchuria. Mao had other ideas. Collusion with Russia or any power wishing to retain Chinese territory would have made him the target of destructive hostil-

ity from a nation that hated all "foreign devils." Moreover
why be a Russian puppet in part of China when he could
become dictator of China?

Communism, in China as in Russia, is nationalism plus
monopoly capitalism directed by an omnipotent bureaucratic
state. This lies at the root of Russo-Chinese rivalry. Chinese
communist nationalism is committed to eliminate foreign in
fluence. Since its establishment in Peking in October, 1949
the new China has expelled Russia from Manchuria and
reduced the Kremlin's economic and political power over
Sinkiang (Chinese Turkestan), an area as large as England
France, and Germany combined, which Moscow, not Chiang
used to rule. China is also wrestling with the Soviet Union in
North Korea where, until the Korean war, Russia was su
preme. Outer Mongolia, a former Chinese province converted
into a political satellite by the tsars and kept so by the Soviet
is likewise a domain of waxing competition between the bear
and the tiger. A vast underdeveloped region of unknown
wealth, Outer Mongolia has only one million inhabitants. It
used to be closed to all foreigners except Soviet citizens. Now
red China is beginning to penetrate, has given technical aid
and trained workers, and would undoubtedly be happy to let
some of her crowded millions spill over into the country and
gradually outnumber the native population.

Stalin foresaw all this. He knew from his own action
during a long career of autocracy that principles did not rule
governors—else how, for instance, could he have signed the
pact with Hitler in 1939 or seized and bled Manchuria in
1945? Stalin expected Mao to behave similarly. He accord
ingly preferred a divided China under noncommunist leader
ship.

When "the Chinese comrades acted quite otherwise" and
defeated Chiang, Stalin plotted to curb Mao's power. North
Korean aggression in 1950, which commenced nine month

after the establishment of the Mao government in Peking, was directed primarily against Japan and the United States. A fortnight's successful campaign against South Korea, as Stalin conceived it, would give Moscow a machine gun pointed at the temple of American power in Japan. But the North Korean conquest of South Korea would also improve Russia's position in Manchuria and vis-à-vis China in general. "A Soviet-dominated Korea," Lieutenant General A. C. Wedemeyer wrote in his report submitted to President Truman on September 9, 1947, "would constitute a serious political and psychological threat to Manchuria, North China, the Ryukyus, and Japan, and hence to United States strategic interests in the Far East." The Korean war was Stalin's double-barreled gambit against America and China.

U.S.-UN armed resistance in Korea spiked his strategy. Somebody had to fight back. Always cautious, ever mindful of the fateful consequences of war on Russian governments (in 1905 as in 1917), Stalin chose not to fight. The Chinese communists did fight, and their impressive military performance resulted in the reassertion of China's power in Manchuria and the ability to question Russia's grip on North Korea.

The nationalism that impelled communist China to oust Russia from Chinese territories would naturally be directed as well against Chiang Kai-shek's positions on the islands of Quemoy and Matsu, situated within four miles of the Chinese coast, and against Formosa. Chiang regards these as part of China. Mao agrees.

Chinese nationalism has likewise engulfed Tibet. Here too the Chiang Kai-shek nationalists and the communist nationalists take one view: both have claimed Chinese sovereignty over the Dalai Lama's theocratic kingdom. But until the advent of the red regime, Tibet was autonomous because the Chinese central government lacked the power to penetrate into those remote Himalayan altitudes. Now China is bring-

ing in ten million Chinese to inundate the four million
Tibetans.

Mao's government has given a further remarkable demonstration of nationalism in Indonesia. There the authorities,
eager to foster a native middle class, ordered the expulsion of
Chinese peddlers, petty shopkeepers, and moneylenders from
rural areas and prodded them to undertake productive pursuits in cities. This was a harsh measure, but it is surely
strange to see the Chinese communist government, author of
far harsher measures at home, defending small-scale capitalists, many of whom left China generations ago and some of
whom are known protagonists of Chiang Kai-shek. Indonesia's foreign minister, Dr. Subandrio, charged in a note
dated December 13, 1959, that members of the Chinese communist embassy in Jakarta had urged Chinese not to obey
President Sukarno's decree banning foreigners from retail
trade in outlying areas. Some of the Chinese thereupon emi-
grated to China, where they became grist to communist propaganda mills. Apparently, Peking's pose as the champion of
patriotic overseas Chinese took precedence over good relations with countries that wished to be friendly.

China's hostile moves along India's borders are likewise
calculated to foment nationalism inside China while an-
tagonizing the biggest noncommunist nation in Asia. Nehru,
burdened with cares and preferring to use limited resources
for economic development rather than armaments, leaned
over backwards and sidewards to remain in Chou En-lai's
good graces. But to no avail. Dictatorships, as far apart and as
different as China is from Cuba, need enemies and create
them if they do not exist. Stalin did that throughout his rule.
So did Hitler. It is Mao's turn. The reason presents no riddle:
the Chinese people are living under tremendous pressures.
To industrialize on a vast scale and in a hurry and to force
half a billion peasants into communes are gigantic ventures

which must be made palatable by constant appeals to patriotism and future benefits: defense of the fatherland and pie in the sky.

True democracy is relaxation. True dictatorship is tension. Tension outside breeds tension inside and vice versa. Mao is not seeking foreign friends to warrant relaxation; he is seeking enemies to justify domestic sacrifices. In such a situation, Mao naturally did not enjoy watching Chairman Khrushchev confer amicably with President Eisenhower, the representative of "American imperialism" which made Chiang Kai-shek possible and "threatened" China in Tibet.

Russia and China are at different stages of development; they are therefore out of step. Soviet citizens see all around them the industrial enterprises, built at such backbending cost, which could render living conditions more comfortable. The Soviet population yearns for relaxation and a better life and discerns no reason why these benefits should elude them when the Soviet Union is so strong and has made so much technological progress. More goods are indeed available to the Soviet consumer, and de-Stalinization, though incomplete, has banished many Stalinist rigors. Mao, on the other hand, tried to persuade the Kremlin to re-enthrone Stalin. For China is in her Stalinist period of accelerated industrialization and uncompromising village communization. The Chinese people can look ahead to long years of privation and strain. Mao's February 27, 1957, promise to let "a hundred flowers" and intellectual liberalism bloom proved empty and disingenuous. The flowers wilted quickly; dissenters were sent away for "corrective labor." Out of step, Moscow and Peking play different tunes.

Lenin formulated the law of "unequal development of capitalist nations" to explain the conflicts among them. The same inequality exists between the two communist colossi. It is manifest in internal as well as foreign policy and may find

expression in personal rivalries too. Today, Mao's reputation
as a theoretician exceeds that of any Soviet leader. Attacks on
theoretical deviations inside the red world often mask dis-
pleasure with political independence. This was the case of
Tito. Mao is another example.

Both Khrushchev and Mikoyan have criticized the Chinese
communes. Mao's prestige among communists would mount
steeply if China, having communized, were recognized as the
pacemaker on the road to the red paradise. Status is important. The Soviets want to be first. "We," a Moscow radio
broadcast boasted on December 30, 1959, "already have socialism and are marching toward communism, whereas the
Chinese are just building socialism which is the initial phase
of communism." The matter was discussed by the supreme
Russian communist body: the Twenty-first Communist Party
Congress. Meeting in Moscow from January 27 to February
5, 1959, it took the view, as stated in the new *History of the
Communist Party of the Soviet Union*, that "all socialist
countries will enter the highest phase of communist society
more or less simultaneously." Admittedly, each socialist
country has its characteristics; "nevertheless, the decisive factor in the progress of all countries toward communism will,
according to the teachings of Marxism-Leninism, be the
[social] laws common to all of them and not their special
phenomena."

Translated from the Aesopian language—a term Lenin
used—into the lingo of the political rialto, this statement
means that farm or even city communes will not carry China
into the communist heaven ahead of Russia. Although collectivized agriculture has yet to prove profitable in Russia and
was an officially admitted failure in Yugoslavia and Poland,
the Kremlin line is that the collective farm—a low social form,
to be sure—still has a long lease on life. Some day it will evolve
into state farms or agricultural factories. But communes are

not envisaged. If the Soviet peasants suspected that China's precedent was soon to be followed in Russia, their resentment might be aroused as it was during the period of compulsory collectivization after 1928. Hence the anticommune statements by Soviet leaders.

Despite the "Soviet-Chinese fraternity" flamboyantly avowed in official communist bloc speeches, competitive Russia is worried by the competition of China. Khrushchev has reflected his concern on more than one occasion. For instance, he said in Budapest on December 1, 1959, "We must make a sensible use of the great advantages of the socialist system and strengthen the world socialist camp in every way. We must not fall behind or go too far ahead. We must, figuratively, synchronize our watches. If the leadership of this or that country becomes conceited, this can only play into the hands of the enemy." None of Russia's European satellites had dared to "go too far ahead." If it ventured to the fore, Khrushchev's word or wink would call it to order. He was troubled by Mao's conceit in pressing on toward communism by means of militarized communes. China's full-speed ahead to the golden gates of communism is not merely a matter of prestige. It involves power. Moscow would like Mao to translate into practice his frequent fiery declarations about "the socialist camp under the leadership of the Soviet Union." But Mao and his comrades did not completely subordinate their views to Moscow's even in the years when they were struggling rebels in Chiang Kai-shek China. Their emphasis in those years was on the organization of disciplined military cadres as the backbone of a largely peasant army. Today they feel strong, xenophobic, and aloof, eager to receive aid and ready to pay for it with verbal obeisances. This does not incline the Kremlin toward economic generosity.

Russia and China are separate nations and different imperialisms whose interests often coincide, occasionally diverge.

The Soviet Union's career of imperialist expansion beyond its 1939 frontiers commenced with the signing of the Stalin-Hitler pact on August 23 of that year. By 1945 Moscow had grabbed vast territories and large populations in Europe and bits and slices in Asia. Ambition fed on the eating; Stalin and Zhdanov, his foreign policy maker, felt that war-weakened Europe offered them an opportunity for further conquests by diplomacy, communist subversion, and the Berlin blockade. The resulting crisis created European defense alliances, notably NATO, with America's invigorating participation, and the Marshall Plan. Thwarted in Europe, Russia in 1949 trained her sights and appetites on Asia, only to be confronted with China's firm "No." Mao had and has no intention of allowing Russia to continue dominating Chinese territory. Nor can China, except in the event of a Soviet-American war which would drastically reduce Russia's population and power, expect to acquire the U.S.S.R.'s thinly inhabited Asiatic regions.

Such a territorial stalemate may, while reflecting frustration, offer the basis for an alliance. Since neither can expand at the other's expense, both seek benefits from co-operation. The Sino-Soviet entente, given China's growing military strength, divides American armed forces between Europe and Asia and is therefore a major advantage to Russia. At considerable expense, the United States props up South Korea, Taiwan, and Vietnam and finds a few weak allies in Southeast and South Asia. But under the menacing shadow of China, backed by Moscow, neither America nor Japan could obtain a safe foothold on the Asian continent. For China, which remembers her recent history of foreign invasion and spheres of influence, this is the political dividend of her alliance with the Soviets.

The internal strains that accompany China's "leap forward" demand a martial climate. The daily fist-shaking at

Formosa, the every-other-day shelling of Quemoy and Matsu, the military subjugation of Tibet, as well as the skirmishes on India's frontier, generate just the right atmosphere of synthetic patriotism in which Mao can justify the burdens and pressures he is imposing on the Chinese people.

It is possible, indeed probable, that the Chinese communist method of solving problems is more militaristic and absolutist than Russia's. Mao has avoided the moderation of Lenin, Stalin, and Khrushchev. Lenin, in 1921, introduced the New Economic Policy (NEP), a coexistence compromise with capitalism, especially in the villages, which lasted until 1928. Red China never had an NEP. After 1928 Stalin collectivized agriculture. But he himself, in his last published work (*The Economic Problems of Socialism in the U.S.S.R.*), called attention to the dual nature of Soviet economy. "At the present time"—1952, he said, "we have two basic forms of socialist production: state-nationalized, and collective-farming which cannot be called nationalized. In state enterprises the means of production as well as the output of the enterprises are national property, whereas in the collective farms the means of production (land, machines) belong to the state but the output is the property of the individual collective farms." Stalin recognized this arrangement as a limitation on the power of the Soviet state and a fault in the Soviet economy. Mao frowned on collective farms which dispose of a part of their crops and instead organized nationwide communes whose produce goes entirely and directly to the government just like the steel from its mills and the coal from its mines. Mao thus imposed a total, absolute solution, whereas even the totalitarian Stalin remained content with a partial solution. Mao knew that Soviet farm collectives, which allowed the peasantry some circumscribed economic freedom, had failed to solve the food problem and created a political and social split in Soviet society between city and countryside.

This coexistence within the Soviet Union of two economic forms which are antagonistic and one of which, collective farming, is ultimately doomed to extinction has its counterpart in Soviet foreign policy. Mao rejects this too. He apparently discerns dangers for communists in a world that they have to share with noncommunists. This approach may be due to a consciousness of present weakness or a confidence in ultimate strength, or both.

Russia, however, does not wish to be dragged into trouble by Peking's military adventurism. Hence the undisguised lack of sympathy Moscow has shown for Mao's policies vis-à-vis India and Indonesia. "We," Khrushchev told the Supreme Soviet in Moscow on October 31, 1959, "deeply regret the incidents that took place recently on the frontier of two states both of which are our friends—the Chinese People's Republic, to which we are bound by indestructible bonds of fraternal friendship, and the Indian Republic, with which we have successfully developed friendly relations." Khrushchev's "deep regret" was a sharp rebuke to Mao. At the least, the statement proves that China does not concert her foreign policy actions with Moscow.

It was after China's frontier incursions into India and her interference in the affairs of Indonesia that Khrushchev set forth on his journey to both India and Indonesia. Mr. K. would surely not have gone to those countries during their disputes with China had he wished to direct China's expansion southward and southeastward. More likely he expected to make hay there while China's sun was not shining. Any major Maoist forward push runs the risk of involving China in a war with the West, and while this would bleed both sides to the profit of Russia, it might also upset the international applecart and end in a total world war, the last thing the Soviet government or Soviet peope want. Khrushchev accordingly warned the Chinese in an address in Peking on

September 30, 1959, against "testing the stability of the capitalist system by force." This, he added, "would be wrong." Throughout that visit the Chinese leaders gave him and his speeches a calculated frigid reception. Apparently "testing the stability of the capitalist system" is Khrushchev's interpretation of China's misguided foreign policy.

"No communist party anywhere, if it really is communist," Khrushchev asserted in Budapest on December 1, 1959, "has ever said that it hopes to achieve its aims through war." This is not true, but it is interesting. At the end of his stay in Indonesia, Khrushchev and President Sukarno signed a joint communiqué on February 28, 1960 (quoted in *Pravda* of the next day), which said in part, "The Chairman of the Council of Ministers of the U.S.S.R. and the President of the Republic of Indonesia emphasized that every disagreement between states should be solved by peaceful means. They are convinced that no use of armaments or the threat of the use of force can solve international problems." China had used arms against India and against Chiang Kai-shek's little isles. Mao might attack Formosa. Khrushchev disapproved. In effect, Moscow was attempting to dictate Mao's foreign policy. China reacted with violence and vigor.

On April 19, 1960, the Chinese telegraphic agency radioed to Europe and Asia the English translation of a 23,000-word article which was to appear a few days later in *Hung-chi* (*Red Star*), the fortnightly organ of the Chinese Communist Party, to commemorate the ninetieth anniversary of Lenin's birth. Subsequently, all daily newspapers in China reproduced part of the original article on their front page. The article correctly emphasized Lenin's view that wars to promote socialism would be just. Speaking in Peking on September 30, 1959, immediately after his visit to America, Khrushchev had thought it advisable to caution China that "if a nation objects it is impossible to impose on it even such a noble and progressive system as socialism." Contradicting Khrushchev, the *Hung-chi* article said that "when the exploiting classes use violence against the people, the possibility of using other means has to be considered; namely, the transition to socialism by nonpeaceful means."

*Hung-chi* devoted a large part of its space to a ferocious attack on President Tito of Yugoslavia. It quoted him as saying at Zagreb on December 12, 1959, "Today the world has entered an epoch in which nations can relax and tranquilly devote themselves to their internal construction tasks. . . . We have entered an epoch in which new questions are on the agenda, not questions of war and peace, but questions of co-operation, economic or otherwise. And where economic co-operation is concerned, there is also the question of economic competition."

This is precisely the position which Khrushchev, and with him the Soviet Communist Party, had taken. For China, Tito is a remote, small fish. In firing a broadside at him, *Hung-chi* was aiming at Khrushchev and the Kremlin. "This renegade," it wrote of Tito, "completely writes off the question of class contradictions and class struggle in the world in an attempt to negate consistent analysis by Marxists-Leninists that our epoch is the epoch of imperialism and proletarian revolution and the epoch of the victory of socialism and communism."

Khrushchev had been calling for a "relaxation of international tensions." But, *Hung-chi* asked, "can the exploited and oppressed people in the imperialist countries 'relax'? Can the people of all the colonies and semicolonies still under imperialist oppression 'relax'? Has the armed intervention led by the U.S. imperialists in Asia, Africa, and Latin America become 'tranquil'?"

"What kind of 'co-operation' is meant?" *Hung-chi* continued, eyes on Khrushchev. "Is it 'co-operation' of the proletariat with the bourgeoisie to protect capitalism? . . . Is it 'co-operation' of socialist countries with capitalist countries to protect the imperialist system in its oppression of the peoples of these countries and the suppression of national liberation wars?"

These "modern revisionists" were challenging Leninism, the Chinese magazine charged: "It is their aim to obliterate the contradiction between the masses of people and the monopoly capitalist class in imperialist countries . . . the contradiction between the socialist system and the imperialist system, and the contradiction between the peace-loving people of the world and the warlike imperialist bloc."

Khrushchev had been led astray. He had taken Eisenhower at his word. He had imagined that imperialist America wanted peace. But "We Marxists," *Hung-chi* proclaimed, "must not base proletarian policy merely on certain passing events or on minute political changes, but must base it on the over-all class contradictions and class struggles of a whole historical epoch. . . . The capitalist-imperialist system absolutely will not crumble of itself. . . . The modern revisionists . . . attempt to overthrow totally the fundamental theories of Marxism-Leninism on a series of questions like violence, war, peaceful coexistence, etc. There are also some people who are not revisionists but well-intentioned persons who sincerely want to be Marxists"—Khrushchev and company?—"but are confused in the face of certain new historical phenomena and thus have some incorrect ideas. For example some of them say that the failure of the U.S. imperialists' policy of atomic blackmail marks the end of violence. While thoroughly refuting the absurdities of the modern revisionists, we should also help these well-intentioned people to correct their erroneous ideas."

This is exactly what China did. During the first week of February, 1960, the high-level Political Consultative Committee of the Warsaw Pact met in Moscow. On February 4,

Moscow *Pravda* printed a list of all the delegates to the conference plus the names of the North Korean and Outer Mongolian observers. The next day *Pravda* published the same list of delegates and observers, but this time it added the name of Kang Sheng, the Chinese observer. Had the Kremlin been unaware of his presence? Everything in official Moscow is strictly protocol. The failure to mention Kang Sheng was a slight, not an oversight. For Kang, an alternate member of the Chinese Politburo, had attended the conference and made a speech, little noticed in the West, not published in Moscow, but distributed in full in English by Hsinhua, the official Chinese telegraphic agency, on February 4. (Is this what forced *Pravda* to include his name on February 5?) Kang vehemently assailed a Russian rapprochement with the West. After paying the normal formal tributes to Khrushchev and indicating that China was at last reconciled to a summit conference between the Soviet Union and the West, Kang Sheng said that, "the United States is not only increasingly isolated day by day politically and militarily, its forces are widely dispersed, and new weapons are lagging behind; economically too it is in an ever more difficult situation." Why, then, was the implied question, seek an understanding with America? There followed, after an interval, a clear criticism of Khrushchev's soft foreign policy. "In its efforts to come to an agreement with the western powers on the conclusion of a German peace treaty and ending the occupation regime in West Berlin," Kang asserted, "the Soviet Union has made many concessions, whereas the western powers have made no appropriate response. The Chinese government and people will steadfastly support the basic stand taken by the Soviet Union and the German Democratic Republic on the solution of the German question."

Through his observer in Moscow, Mao was obviously

throwing his support to East Germany and the critics of Khrushchev, who are known to exist in the top leadership of the Soviet Communist Party, against the official policy of "peaceful coexistence" which Kang never mentioned. He did, however, speak of disarmament as "a long-term and complicated struggle between us and imperialism," and served notice on the West and the Kremlin that "any international agreements arrived at without the formal participation of the Chinese People's Republic and the signature of its delegate cannot, of course, have any binding force on China."

Having thus disposed of Berlin and disarmament, the two crucial items on the agenda of the summit conference, the Chinese spokesman pointedly warned that "United States ruling circles . . . aimed . . . at wrecking the unity of the peace forces of the world . . . they are even dreaming of a 'peaceful evolution' in the socialist countries." This was a hint that Khrushchev would be guilty of this very sin if he came to an understanding with "American imperialism," "the principal enemy," said Kang, "of world peace [whose] nature cannot be changed." He also informed his Soviet bloc audience that an "over-all settlement of the overseas Chinese question still needs a certain period of time and may go through some ups and downs."

Mao was proclaiming his own intransigence in foreign affairs and recommending it to Moscow. Madame Sun Yat-sen, deputy chairman of the Chinese government, reinforced this message in an article which, significantly, appeared in the Moscow *Pravda* of February 14, 1960. It repeated several of Kang Sheng's contentions and added a snide reference to President Eisenhower traveling "halfway around the world wearing the mask of an envoy of peace." Khrushchev, on the other hand, had been testifying in public to the sincerity of Eisenhower's efforts for peace.

All this happened with a soothing musical accompaniment of hymns to eternal devotion. Mao makes lavish kowtows to Moscow and admits the Kremlin's primacy in the world communist movement. Moscow proclaims, known facts to the contrary notwithstanding, that "there is not a single international issue of any significance" on which it disagrees with Peking. China and Russia naturally wish to erase the widespread impression that they are washing their soiled linen in public. They even plug the keyhole of the laundry door to prevent sensitive ears from catching rumbles of quarrels. Communists believe in manipulating minds—as Pavlov manipulated the brains of dogs. Hence the incessant advertising of frictionless relations between the two big communist countries; some people will be fooled.

An interesting and significant parallel has been drawn between Khrushchev's and Malenkov's relations with China. Malenkov, on succeeding Stalin as prime minister in March, 1953, followed a moderate foreign policy. In the very month that Malenkov became number one Soviet leader, Prime Minister Kim Il Sung of North Korea and Chinese Premier Chou En-lai spoke in favor of a Korean truce which Stalin had impeded. On April 1, 1953, Molotov said, "This proposal . . . allows for an armistice in Korea." Peace in Korea was Malenkov's achievement. In other ways too, Malenkov also sought improved relations with the West. He declared on March 6, 1954, that an atomic war would destroy civilization; previously communists had alleged it would destroy capitalism only. In the summer of 1954 Malenkov successfully pressed Peking to enter into negotiations in Geneva with a view to the settlement of the Indo-China war. Malenkov likewise made a big cut in the military budget of the Soviet Union and discouraged large-scale aid for China. His policy envisaged an expansion of consumers' goods available to the Soviet public. Khrushchev, the Russian army, and

China therefore had a common interest in the downfall of Malenkov, who "resigned" on February 8, 1955. On a motion of Khrushchev, the Supreme Soviet elected Nikolai A. Bulganin, theretofore minister of defense, as the new prime minister. Marshal Zhukov was promoted from assistant minister to minister of defense. The army had its reward.

Today Khrushchev, party secretary and prime minister, champions "peaceful coexistence," wishes to broaden the supply of consumers' commodities, and is having his difficulties with bellicose China. Notwithstanding an aversion to the dark and dubious science of Kremlinology, one might hazard the guess that there is in the top Soviet leadership a faction which sets more store by good relations with China than with the West and thinks there is too much Malenkov in Khrushchev; it would advocate more Stalinism at home in order to align Russia with China. Khrushchev, however, apparently believes he can have his China and sup with America, and borrow from Malenkov and yet remain Khrushchev and number one.

The Chinese communists, however, gave Khrushchev no peace. For weeks they cried "revisionism" every time he spoke, à la Malenkov, of the destructiveness and insanity of nuclear war and the possibility of avoiding it. Every time he mentioned coexistence they tried to pillory him in a brace of Lenin quotations. Finally Khrushchev, weary of the game, resorted to the bull-in-the-china-shop manner which he always keeps in reserve. Addressing a gathering in Bucharest attended by the highest officials of all communist countries (except China, which sent an observer), Khrushchev exclaimed on June 21, 1960, "Comrades, we must not now repeat mechanically what was said many decades ago by Vladimir Ilyich Lenin." History was marching on. There might come a day when "capitalism will survive only in a few small countries, as small perhaps, moreover, as, for instance, the button on a jacket. Well? Will it be necessary in such conditions to look up in the book what Vladimir Ilyich Lenin said altogether correctly for his period and simply repeat that wars are inevitable as long as capitalist countries exist?" He went even further. "We live in a time," he asserted, "when Marx, Engels, and Lenin are not with us. If we behave like children who, learning to read, pronounce words letter for letter, we will not get very far."

It is probably too much to hope that Khrushchev's pronouncement will finally liberate him and other communists from the straitjacket of obsolete absolute doctrine. Nevertheless, the declaration could prove epoch-making. It indicates that time is chipping away at the hitherto unquestioned "truths" of communist dogma and may ultimately chip it into a new shape more consonant with twentieth-century needs. It was, significantly, Chinese bellicosity, raising the specter of a war into which Russia would be dragged, that provoked Khrushchev's pioneering statement. Moscow is probably painfully aware that China, with her great and waxing population and her industrial underdevelopment, fears war less than Russia and other developed nations. For this reason the Kremlin would logically be averse to helping Mao toward the possession of atomic and hydrogen bombs.

Khrushchev's revisionist lance found a chink in the Chinese communists' Marxist armor and he must have brought other weapons into the fray, for within a few weeks he forced them to pay at least lip service to his pet theme of peaceful coexistence. Yet he offered them plenty of balm in the form of ferocious attacks on President Eisenhower, the American army, and American policies. He combined advocacy of coexistence with denunciations of the United States, the chief partner in his proposed coexistence scheme, and tried to give this contradictory stance a semblance of plausibility by saying talks could be reopened with Eisenhower's successor in the White House, thus implying that all would be forgiven once the President who accepted responsibility for the U-2's incursion into Soviet territory had retired to his farm and golf course. Simultaneously, however, Khrushchev did everything he could to please Mao and antagonize America: he volunteered to protect Cuba against U.S. aggression, which he knew had not occurred and would not occur unless he provoked it, and he placed the same missiles at the disposal of Lumumba against United Nations "aggression" in the Congo. Moscow also kept the West Berlin bludgeon handy to use over the head of the new U.S. President. This warmed-up cold war satisfied red China's taste for trouble and perhaps stilled her legitimate fears of a bridge between America and Russia which would weaken the link between her and Moscow.

Yet it was characteristic of Khrushchev and a reflection of his *niet* and *da* (no and yes) strategy that after torpedoing the May, 1960, summit conference he went from Paris to East Berlin and disappointed his few friends there by announcing, contrary to many expectations, that he would not sign the separate treaty with East Germany. Why? Several explanations have been advanced. He was not ready to throw overboard the policy of coexistence. He had authored and promoted it. To declare it bankrupt would have exposed his mistake and weakened his position in the Kremlin. The signing of the treaty with East Germany and the consequent threat to West Berlin, moreover, would have consolidated the West even more than Khrushchev's performance at the abortive Paris summit conference. Khrushchev did not know how far the West would go in defense of West Berlin, and he wished to avoid war. Stalin's provocative acts in Europe between 1946 and 1948 had been responsible for the Truman Doctrine, Marshall Plan, and NATO, for Russia's headache from then to now. Khrushchev hoped to avoid the despot's blunders. Finally, Moscow, and particularly the Soviet military, lacked sufficient trust in the East German army to enhance its power by transferring to it the function of checking traffic between West Berlin and West Germany which the Russian forces of occupation were exercising. Who could know whether someday the East German and West German armies might not come to an agreement at the expense of the Soviets? It was no secret to anyone that the East German officers' corps contained many nationalists and nazis thinly disguised as communists.

For the safety of his own career and for the safeguarding of Russia's imperial interest, Khrushchev refrained from signing the East German treaty. He thus held the coexistence door ajar to have a look at the new American President and at political developments in Europe. He thus discouraged while encouraging China. He also fed the Soviet people's yearning for true peace and a better life through disarmament and improved relations with the West. The Soviet dictators may have their split views on China. The Soviet citizen knows that red China bodes him no good.

There are so many soft spots in the Asian underbelly—among them Laos, Cambodia, Vietnam, and so forth—that the Chinese tiger continues to prowl and the Russian bear continues to growl. They need each other yet do not trust each other. Chou En-lai had paid his respects to Khrushchev's coexistence formula, yet Moscow was apparently not convinced, for it kept saying to Peking (the *Izvestia* of August 13, 1960, for instance): "There are some people who draw absolutely absurd conclusions from the recent international complications." They think "recent developments have proved that the nature of imperialism remains unchanged, and if this is so there can be no peaceful coexistence of two systems, no prevention of war. . . . Only dogmatists can reason in such a way." Those, *Izvestia* charged, "who wish to substitute a dead dogma for the developing, living teaching of Marxism-Leninism" are guilty of "blasphemy" when they quote Lenin.

These ideological squabbles hide a big truth: Moscow is afraid of Mao. Late in the summer of 1960 a Moscow correspondent of the London *New Statesman and Nation* reported about a "massive" exodus from China of Russian students and industrial specialists; "the gist of their reports is that China, in its present mood of arrogant chauvinism, is a danger to world peace." Chinese nationalism and Russian nationalism clash just as Russian nationalism and Yugoslav nationalism clashed. Their communism is not the essence.

This comes clearly to the surface when a Yugoslav enters the fray. In 1960, Edvard Kardelj, number-two man in Yugoslavia and a noted communist theoretician, wrote a book entitled *Socialism and War,* which dealt with the heart of the Russo-Chinese debate. Moscow *Pravda,* in a long article on September 2, 1960, took him severely to task and charged him with "whitewashing the aggressive actions of American imperialism." The "theoretical fall from grace" of this "apostle of Yugoslav revisionism," *Pravda* wrote, led him so far from the "Marxist-Leninist theory on questions of war" that he thinks "war is inherent not only in the nature of imperialism but also in the nature of socialist countries." According to Kardelj, as quoted by *Pravda,* "no one socialist country becomes automatically immune to egoistic tendencies and acts only because it is socialist." Kardelj asserts that "classic Marxists did not exclude the possibility of a socialist state conducting an unjust war." For, says Kardelj, a socialist country may have negative characteristics such as the desire for hegemony and "the tendency to conduct reactionary wars." The *Pravda* article condemns Kardelj for these statements and for suggesting, further, that "antagonistic contradictions" may exist between socialist states. Kardelj implies, say the two authors of the *Pravda* article, that communist China is an aggressor. For his stand they brand him "an attorney of American imperialism." "It was his duty," they declare, "to show in his very first lines that imperialism, and above all American imperialism, is the only carrier of the danger of war, is alone guilty of causing international tensions." Instead, the Yugoslav theoreticians "attempt to shed doubt on the peaceloving character of the foreign policy of the socialist camp," and Kardelj, write the *Pravda* authors, even rejects the thesis that "the fact of a socialist country conducting a war is the sole criterion of its being a just war." Kardelj even put the word "just" in quotation marks, *Pravda* complained.

Kardelj's book criticized communist states for the wish to dominate—"hegemony-ism," *Pravda* called it. The Yugoslav showed that one communist country sometimes tries to force its form of communism on another communist country. He ought to know; this is what Russia endeavored to do to Yugoslavia, but Tito rebuffed the Kremlin colonialists. He wanted his country to be independent, with himself as master in his own home, and, being a Central European, he intended to introduce a system which, while still one-party communism, was closer than Russia or China to the twentieth century of the West. One of the reasons for the gulf between Yugoslav and Chinese communism is the distance between West and East, a distance that can be translated into centuries until the centuries are overcome by technological progress. Russia is nearer the West than China, yet not so relaxed and liberal as Yugoslavia. Kardelj, therefore, could not blame only "American imperialism" for world tension. In all logic, he had to blame those who believed that capitalism was original sin, that socialist states could do no evil, and who, consequently, regarded wars waged by communists as "just" wars. It was the Chinese communists, in their controversy with Moscow, who enunciated the proposition of just wars. Khrushchev feared the practical consequences of such a stand: China might go to war. But the moment a leading Yugoslav communist intervened in the debate, *Pravda* sided with the Chinese warmongers. On two basic propositions, "just war," and the sole guilt of America, *Pravda,* spokesman of Soviet communism, having been provoked by Kardelj, backed Mao.

All this, however, is on the level of ideology—theology, one might even call it. But ideology does not interest Khrushchev deeply. Power interests him. China is already Russia's rival for power and will become more so as the years pass. At moments it must be Moscow's nightmare.

The bear and the tiger are at such odds that they can no longer conceal the fact. In August, 1960, a world congress of orientalists assembled in Moscow. The Soviets had announced in advance that a large Chinese delegation would be present. No Chinese appeared. . . . On October 1, 1960, communist China celebrated the anniversary of its birth. Contrary to precedent, no Soviet delegation participated. Nobody came from any of Russia's satellites—except puny Albania. These are astounding developments. Sino-Soviet relations have taken on the aspects of a real and deep struggle.

The Russo-Chinese cold war is a circle of trouble within the global cold war and calls for a reassessment of the latter. As Yugoslav communism is easier to deal with than Soviet communism, so Soviet communism is easier to deal with than Chinese communism. Khrushchev is no Mao, and Khrushchev's successor will be of a younger and therefore less sour vintage than he. Politics is the science of the lesser evil. There is no perfection.

Even China must not be pushed out of the pale. By barring communist China from the UN the United States has gained nothing but the enmity of many Asian and other countries. There is good reason to believe that Mao China does not want UN membership and would not accept it unless Formosa

were excluded. The U.S. should allow red China to join the
UN, insist on Formosa remaining in that body as a separate
state without vain ambitions to reconquer the mainland, and
persuade Chiang Kai-shek or his successor to withdraw from
the tiny islands of Quemoy and Matsu which are not necessary to the defense of Formosa and are only a source of international friction. For Chiang the islands are a pawn in his
game to stay in power against the wishes of many Formosans.

The problem of United States diplomatic recognition of
communist China is more complicated because it has become
a football in American domestic politics. It involves the debate over who "lost" China. Chiang Kai-shek lost China because he did not introduce the indispensable social reforms;
he looked backward instead of forward. The United States
ought not to look backward. Red China is there and will be a
growing factor in world affairs. In diplomacy it is best to be
present. U.S. recognition of the Soviet Union bore no fruit—
until 1941 when American national interests dictated military
aid to Stalin to defeat Hitler. Nothing is permanent in world
affairs except permanent change.

## chapter 5

---

# *Khrushchev*

It was reported recently that when Chairman Nikita S. Khrushchev visited New York he told Governor Nelson Rockefeller of his intention, before the Bolshevik Revolution, to emigrate to America. He would have been a big success. He might have become mayor of Chicago, president of General Motors, boss of the Teamsters trade union, or head of a giant advertising firm, for he is the world's best advertiser.

Khrushchev has vigor and humor, a quick mind, an excellent memory, a genius for debate, a faith in himself, and a knowledge of human weaknesses. He is temperamental. "I have a somewhat restless character and I am a blunt man," he admitted on September 25, 1959. He enjoys verbal ju-jitsu and often downs his opponent. He likes to meddle and criticize. On his busy trip to America he went out of his way to visit the model corn farm of Mr. Roswell Garst in Iowa. Reporting about it to Muscovites on September 28, 1959, he said, "I found some shortcomings. The corn is planted too densely, and I, of course, called his attention to this, friendly like." He did not reveal Mr. Garst's reply. At President Eisenhower's Gettysburg farm Khrushchev discovered that "it is not a rich farm and the soil there is not too good," and he so informed Eisenhower. Yet during many years this voluble, opinionated, ebullient man with a low boiling point swallowed Stalin's humiliating insults, exercised restraint, and respected the cruel rules of the totalitarian game. For answering back would have meant a bullet in the back of the neck.

There is evidence that Khrushchev (and Mikoyan) hated and hate Stalin. Though he delivers scores of speeches a year, Khrushchev never hints that Stalin, who ruled in Russia from 1924 to 1953, even existed. He demonstratively omits Stalin's name when he might properly include it. For instance, a 21-gun salute was fired in honor of Khrushchev as he was leaving the United States from the Andrews air force base near Washington. He told about it at a meeting in Vladivostok on October 6, 1959. "After the first volley," Khrushchev stated, "I thought, 'That one's for Karl Marx. The second volley—for Friedrich Engels. The third volley— for Vladimir Ilyich Lenin.'" Here one would expect him to mention Stalin. No. "The fourth—for His Majesty the Working Class, the Toiling people." Therewith the list ended.

"Stalin held us in his hand," Mikoyan said with bitterness when I asked him in 1956 why he had not done anything against Stalin's tyranny in the 1930's. Helpless, he had contemplated suicide. "And at the end of Stalin's life," he added, "I was about to be executed."

Both Mikoyan and Khrushchev bided their time and took revenge on the image of Stalin. Khrushchev broke the idol and clambered over the pieces to the pinnacle of the Soviet pyramid. Some would say that Khrushchev is the most powerful politician on earth—a remarkable achievement for a poor coal miner's son who began his "professional" career as a shepherd boy and later became a locksmith and worked in the Donetz coal mines.

An official biography says Nikita Sergeivich Khrushchev was born on April 17, 1894, in a village called Kalinovka in the province of Kursk in Central Russia. Though he became the communist chief of the Ukraine and, as he himself once declared, mastered enough of the Ukrainian language to understand it and to speak it poorly, he is a Great Russian. His father was "a landless and propertyless peasant" who, like many of his class, worked in the mines when there was no work in the village. Nikita had little schooling. He did, however, attend the village Orthodox Church services. "In my youth," he told a Vienna audience on July 2, 1960, "I was religious; in fact, the priest praised me for my knowledge of the Bible." The boy memorized biblical stories which he used as parables to illustrate communist propaganda theses when he became the number one Soviet leader. Noah and the ark served him as a case of the coexistence of the pure and the impure, the clean and the unclean, the communists and the capitalists. "The people who disrupted the conference," he said in Bucharest on June 21, 1960, after he had disrupted the Paris summit conference in May, "now shed crocodile tears. They mourn as Judas mourned in betraying Christ." But, he added, "We do not live in the times when the legend of Christ was formulated." Nikita had left far behind him the beliefs of his churchgoing youth. His gods were nineteenth-century men.

Herding sheep and cows, working in the mines and at a coke furnace, Khrushchev did not learn to read and write until he was twenty years old, during the first year of the First World War. In 1918 he joined the Russian Communist Party and from then to 1920 fought the antibolshevik Whites as a soldier in Budenny's famous rough-riding Red Cavalry Army. He remained a rank-and-file communist until 1925, when he was appointed a party organizer and commenced his climb to leadership. A biography of Khrushchev might be subtitled "From the Coal Pit to the Kremlin Peak."

Everything Khrushchev is and has he owes to the Soviet

regime, and he naturally glorifies it. Just so, millions of Americans who rose from poverty to power or from slums to wealth praise the American system unstintingly. None of Khrushchev's predecessors at the Soviet summit, neither Lenin nor Stalin nor Malenkov, ever described the country's achievements with such gusto. There is, to be sure, more to describe, and Khrushchev makes the most of it. But one imagines that he would have done a better job than the earlier leaders even with the more limited material at their disposal, for he is the born propagandist. In America his kind are called "public relations counsels." They sell automobiles, cigarettes, plastic girdles, and company virtues. Khrushchev sells socialism and he could give pointers to Madison Avenue in the craft which he has raised to an art. His qualifications for the task are multiple: a conviction that what was good for Nikita is good for the world; a closed mind to the wares of the competitor; and a lusty pleasure in competition. Also, his concepts are simple and primitive and he expresses them endlessly with unflagging zest as though he had never before uttered them and his audience had never before heard them. This, as any TV viewer or radio listener or newspaper reader can testify, is the first law of advertising.

Khrushchev's advertising methods depend for success on an unabashed concealment of half, sometimes of three thirds, of the truth. Thus in July, 1960, he declaimed before innumerable Austrians who knew better that Austria received her independence and release from foreign occupation thanks to the Soviet government's agreement to the State Treaty of 1955. This was true. He did not, however, say that the Western powers had urged Moscow to sign the treaty in 1945 and in literally hundreds of conferences between 1945 and 1955. Moscow finally capitulated in 1955. The fact, therefore, is that Russia delayed Austria's independence and freedom from occupation for an entire decade.

Similarly, Khrushchev boasts on innumerable occasions that, beginning in 1961, the Soviet government plans to introduce a seven-hour day and for some—miners and minors —a six-hour day. Most human beings will applaud this innovation and hope that it also means a five-day workweek. But millions in the western world who have enjoyed a forty-hour week since the 1930's or the 1940's or 1950's will marvel at his temerity in claiming that Russia will soon have the shortest workday.

Courageously ignoring facts, Khrushchev takes every opportunity to declare that the Soviet Union is a democracy. He told the Indian parliament, for instance, on February 11, 1960, "Is it not the unity of our people and the democracy of the Soviet system of government that is seen from the fact that there have been no instances of prosecution for political reasons in our country during the past several years?" The surcease from terror "during the past several years" is highly welcome. But Khrushchev and all other Soviet leaders and every Soviet channel of communication claimed that Russia was a democracy throughout the period of draconic Stalinist terror. Communists contend that the Soviet system is democratic by its very nature. Here Khrushchev was arguing that the end of political prosecutions had made the Soviet Union a democracy. Is this negative phenomenon, however desirable, sufficient proof?

At a meeting in Vienna on July 2, 1960, Khrushchev commented at length on a speech by Senator Fulbright several days earlier criticizing the Eisenhower administration's handling of the U-2 incident and especially President Eisenhower's acceptance of personal responsibility for the flight. This was the kind of voice of America, Khrushchev said, that he liked to hear and it was being broadcast throughout the Soviet Union. When Mr. Khrushchev can decide which voice, which articles, speeches, novels, plays, and paintings can and cannot be made available to the Soviet people, his country is not a democracy. If he or one of his colleagues could have criticized Stalin or if one of his colleagues could today criticize him on such basic political issues as Senator Fulbright criticized Eisenhower he would be entitled to call Russia a democracy. Apparently Khrushchev does not wish to see and believes his audience does not understand that in praising Fulbright's American democracy he is exposing the dictatorial nature of the Soviet system.

On a television program in New York on October 9, 1960, Chairman Khrushchev declared that he believed in the independence of all peoples, that any of the Soviet republics— the Ukraine, Belorussia, Georgia, Armenia, etc.—could secede from the Soviet Union if it wished. This fantasy might have been shattered with a simple, single-word question: "How?" Would the Soviet government permit an unhindered plebiscite in the Ukraine or Georgia on the issue of secession? Free voting is not allowed on less important issues. Would the Soviet authorities countenance propaganda for secession? Perpetrators of such propaganda would immediately be imprisoned as "reactionary fascist imperialists instigated by western capitalism." In the 1920's and 1930's, Stalin purged and repurged Ukrainians, communists as well as noncommunists, suspected of Ukrainian nationalism and separatism. As master of the Ukraine, Khrushchev himself stamped out anyone remotely inclined toward Ukrainian secession. Yet with serious mien and his usual vigor, he told his American viewer audience that the Ukraine, etc. were free to secede. (As free as Hungary in 1956.) He is too intelligent to believe what he said. But in the First World War, Lenin preached self-determination and the right of secession for all the nations of the world, the right of secession is written into the Soviet Constitution, and Mr. Khrushchev repeats the words of the theory-without-reality in the expectation that some will be fooled. The gulf between creed and deed is very broad in the Soviet Union.

Mr. Khrushchev's roots, like the roots of Bolshevism, reach back into tsarist Russia. He knows more about dictatorship than he does about democracy. Yet he quickly learned how to take advantage of freedom. At the United Nations Assembly session which began in September, 1960, he twice heckled Prime Minister Macmillan and thumped his desk whenever any other speaker displeased him. It is not difficult to imagine what would happen to a Soviet person who did something similar in the Soviet Union. Because Dag Hammarskjöld, acting under UN instructions, had, in effect, blocked Russian expansion into the Congo, Khrushchev wanted to purge him (send him to Outer Mongolia?), asked for his resignation, and tried to emasculate the UN. Bolshevik strategy, since Lenin demonstrated it masterfully in 1917 against the Kerensky government, is the undermining of an administration prior to capturing it. After seizing power, the Soviets purge. How frustrating for Khrushchev not to be able to purge Hammarskjöld. That is the way a Kremlin boss deals with opposition. This is the system Khrushchev likes and offers free to other countries.

Khrushchev is the practical, unself-critical businessman in politics. We do not know how much Marxist theory he has mastered. But he certainly read the 1848 Marx and Engels *Communist Manifesto,* and from it he borrowed the rhythm method of history. "Feudalism existed and was succeeded by capitalism," he said at the National Press Club in Washington, D.C. ". . . As Marx, Engels, and Lenin proved, communism will succeed capitalism. We believe in this." Adherents of a religious sect occasionally parade in city streets carrying signs with the legend "Repent, the end of the world is near." Figuratively, Khrushchev wanders from country to country with a placard reading "Beware, the end of capitalism is near." Khrushchev's rhythm method assumes the death of the old and the birth of something totally different. Recent events show that the old can, by changing, enjoy a second life.

Facts, however, have no chance against faith, and Khrushchev says, "We believe in this." Khrushchev's certainty that the rhythm of history will make communism the heir of capitalism rests on the thesis that communism is more enlightened, progressive, and creative. In a letter dated December 3, 1957, and addressed to C. Rajagopalachari, a venerable leader of independent India, Khrushchev mentioned "the achievements in Soviet science and technology" and asserted that "they show the progress made by a people that has won its freedom from capitalist slavery." This is a recurrent theme. On May 15, 1958, he announced the launching of a third Soviet sputnik weighing 1,327 kilograms and compared it derisively with the "orange-sized American artificial satellites." Again, speaking in Halle, East Germany, on July 8, 1958, he said, "The Americans launched three of their orange-sized sputniks. But their sputniks are a hundred times smaller than the third Soviet sputnik. And what does this imply? It implies that Soviet science has surpassed American achievements. That is a big victory for us, comrades. It is an expression of the will of the working class and the wisdom of the communist movement."

Chairman Khrushchev has been going up and down the earth handing out tomato-sized replicas of the Soviet emblem that was deposited on the moon. President Eisenhower received one, as did President de Gaulle, and President Sukarno. Such pride is normal. It is even legitimate, given the world we live in and Moscow's attitude toward competitive

existence, to use sputniks as military-diplomatic demon-
ations. The Soviets fired the moon rocket on the eve of
rushchev's visit to America, and a very heavy satellite
st before the May, 1960, Paris summit conference, which
ver started on account of Khrushchev's theatrical tantrum
er the U.S. U-2 spy-in-the-sky incident. Russians like to
gotiate from strength—as who doesn't? The U-2 was a
nbolic robber of Soviet strength. Its deep penetration
to Soviet territory suggested that jet bombers carrying
clear bombs might have done likewise. In view of this
miliation, Khrushchev felt that he could not confer with
e western heads of state until he forced upon Eisenhower
equal humiliation reflecting fears and weakness. Moscow
nsidered that the U-2 had diminished Russia's weight at
e scheduled conference. Khrushchev draws an equal sign be-
een weight and strength and prestige. "The weight of the
ree artificial earth satellites placed in orbit by the Soviet
nion," he told a Soviet-Czechoslovak friendship meeting
Moscow on July 12, 1958, "is a symbol of our country's
ight in international affairs." Russia has a tradition of
ight-worship. In the Moscow Kremlin today stands the
-ton "Tsar-Cannon" cast in 1586. Likewise to be seen on
e ground in the Kremlin is the eighteenth-century "Tsar-
ll," the heaviest bell in the world, weighing two hundred
ns. In science, however, weight and size are not synony-
ous with utility. One leaves it to the physicists to deter-
ine whether the heavier Russian satellites made a greater
ientific contribution than the lighter and more numerous
merican varieties: Pioneer V, for instance, weighing only
pounds, which answered questions from the earth after
aching almost ten million miles into space; Tiros I, weigh-
g 270 pounds, which circled the planet for months carry-
g two television cameras—one capable of photographing an
ea of 640,000 square miles, the second an area of 900

square miles; Discoverer XIII which, while orbiting
space, ejected a 300-pound capsule fished out of the Paci
by the navy; the 100-foot balloon called Echo II, whi
bounced back to earth messages sent from the earth; Va
guard 1, a grapefruit-sized satellite, which reported by rad
on October 2, 1960, that it had completed its 10,000th orl
around the earth and was still circling; etc., etc. Surely t
criterion is not weight.

As to the relationship between sputniks and "freedo
from capitalist slavery," it might be helpful to recall th
great astronomers, city builders, and architects worked f
ancient oriental despots, that through the ages tyrants ha
fostered science, that Russia under tsarist autocracy pr
duced eternal literature and music, and that *Dr. Zhivag*
the Soviet Union's finest novel, could not be published the

Mr. Khrushchev, orbiting around the globe and traveli
far and wide at home, is the heaviest sputnik of all. F
boasts about Russia's achievements and "the wisdom of tl
communist movement" to boost his own prestige and pow
He won international renown with the secret speech at tl
Twentieth Communist Party Congress in February, 195
condemning Stalin. When I asked Anastas I. Mikoyan
Moscow in the summer of 1956 why the speech had not be
printed in the Soviet Union, he replied, "It is too early
Apparently it is still too early. In fact, the existence of tl
address used to be denied angrily by Kremlin spokesme
But now the biography of Khrushchev in the *Great Sovi*
*Encyclopedia* states that "on February 25, at a secret sessic
of the congress, he delivered a report 'On the Cult of Pc
sonality and its Consequences.'" The consequences we
drastic and tragic and a crushing criticism, which the Krer
lin refused to recognize, of the undemocratic system th
allowed it to happen and could no nothing about it. Toda
moreover, Khrushchev has in turn made himself the obje

of a cult of personality. The Soviet book *Face to Face with
America,* written about Khrushchev's stay in the U.S.A. by
twelve Soviet editors and journalists including the editor
of *Pravda,* and his son-in-law, the editor of *Izvestia,* is full
of worshipful adulation of the Soviet Chairman, and, inci-
dentally, just as full of anti-American venom. The Soviet
press daily drips with his praise. A new poster to be seen in
Moscow shows Khrushchev by the side of the Lenin whom
he never knew. The March-April, 1960, issue of *Istoriya
SSSR (The History of the U.S.S.R.),* published in Moscow
and entirely devoted to the ninetieth anniversary of Lenin's
birth, starts with a nineteen-page article on Lenin and ends
with a four-line quotation from Khrushchev which is a color-
less communist cliché. The second article devotes twenty
pages to the brief Lenin period of Soviet history, half a page
to Stalin's twenty-seven years in power without mentioning
his name, and then passes to the Khrushchev era where
Khrushchev is copiously quoted. Likewise the third article
on "Lenin and the Foreign Policy of the Soviet State" gives
eight pages to Lenin's six years in office, one page to Stalin's
reign—again without using his name—and five pages to the
Khrushchev administration. This is the latest pattern: Lenin
canonized, Stalin ignored, Khrushchev exalted.

Stalin, the loathed paranoiac, needed the orgy of saccha-
rine glorification to make him the officially "beloved" father
figure. Khrushchev, who is not noticeably neurotic, needs
the new cult to efface the widely held view that though he
is an improvement on Stalin he lacks the dignity and stature
to be Russia's foremost leader. His cult of personality also
serves a political purpose. He has opponents in the Kremlin
and more in China, and the two forces wash each other's
hands. Since Khrushchev can deal with neither through secret
police executions, he appeals over the heads of inner power
groups to the public. This use of popularity to advance

policy is unique in the Soviet Union's history. Lenin ap
pealed to the party. Stalin appealed to no one. Khrushchev
irrepressible and gifted salesman, courts the party and th
people. This phenomenon could, in time, become the feebl
embryo of democracy in the dinosaur of dictatorship.

Russians have ever loved their country and hated thei
governments. Even the Jews and others who fled from perse
cution in the nineteenth century remembered Mother Ru
sia with tender longing. They felt a nostalgia for her steppes
rivers, and trees, for her language and literature. The
recited her poetry and sang her songs. Russia has a savag
strength, the frustrated power of a giant chained. The natio
possesses some uncertain, dark, brooding quality, like a vol
cano always threatening to vomit forth black lava. The gian
can murder and weep, burn and build, worship and scof
obey and obstruct. Bolshevism undertook to tame him
gouge out his eyes and cut out his tongue, and hitch a re
cart to him so he would drag it under the knout. Ivan th
Terrible did something similar; Peter the Great likewise
Russia is big and heavy and her roads are rutted and muddy
Men must have mighty wills and little squeamishness t
budge her great lumbering body. Lenin was ruthless an
maniacally single-tracked. Stalin had steel nerves, no hear
and a monster's brain. He transformed the cart into
caterpillar tractor and drove it over fields of living flesh
They buried his mummy in marble by the side of hol
Lenin, then called him a butcher and blunderer yet kep
his remains in the mausoleum from the top of which the
review the marching millions. Lenin-idolized and Stalin
reviled form the base from which they rule. Now they hav
discovered that the giant has kept part of his sight and ca
mumble and think. He will work when whipped and worl
when rewarded. The age of the jet and the age of the knou

are in conflict. Power without people is an anachronism, an impossibility. So Khrushchev has flung open the gates of the Kremlin in a symbolic gesture and stepped down from its parapets into the streets to talk a lot and listen a little.

Khrushchev's primary task is to convince the Soviet population (and the world) that communism must win in the coexistence war with capitalism. "Up to now," he told the meeting of the Socialist Unity Congress of East Germany on July 11, 1958, "socialism has been completed in only one country—in the Soviet Union." China, in other words, was not yet socialist, much less communist. But "we"—the Soviet Union—"are now advancing successfully to a communist society." He had given the proof two days earlier to another East German audience when he reported that the next Soviet harvest would be good, with the result that "we shall be able to eat both bread and sausage and have enough to spare for beer." To German ears, at least, bread and wurst and beer spell capitalist poverty.

Some months later, on November 3, 1958, Khrushchev spoke at a large factory in Leningrad, Russia's second city, and rounded out the picture of socialism. Again he referred to the "exceedingly good" harvest. The quotation is from a Russian-language Soviet book, entitled *For Victory in Peaceful Competition with Capitalism*, which appeared in New York in 1960 in exact translation with a special introduction by Mr. Khrushchev. This harvest, he declared, "means that now we shall have enough grain to bake brown bread, and white bread, and make pancakes, and dumplings, and still have enough left over as a reserve." He asserted that the country had also had "marked successes . . . in the production of milk and meat."

"Do you have enough milk in Leningrad?" Khrushchev asked.

"Voices: We do.

"Khrushchev: Perhaps you don't want to let down your leadership, or do you really have milk?

"Voices: We do. We do."

Khrushchev then said that the party had undertaken "to solve the housing problem in ten to twelve years. . . .

"Voices: Couldn't this term be reduced?

"Khrushchev: That depends on you, on all our people, and explained that if they worked harder the prospects would be brighter."

Khrushchev obviously keeps in contact with his public, something Stalin never did. From January, 1928, till his death in March, 1953, Stalin did not visit a village. Khrushchev knows conditions. Yet in reply to Polish journalists' questions on March 10, 1958, he blithely declared, "The national income, which is the most general index of the people's well-being, has risen in the U.S.S.R. fourteenfold per head of population since 1913." If people's well-being is synonymous with national income, we must assume that a workers' family which lived in one room under the Tsar now has fourteen rooms; each child that had one pair of shoes now has fourteen; every woman who possessed one dress in 1913 now owns fourteen. How wonderful but, alas, how untrue. In the United States, on the other hand, Khrushchev said to M. Groussard, *Le Figaro* correspondent, on March 19, 1958, millions of people "can die from want and privation or drag out a miserable existence and none of the millionaires and billionaires will be worried about it."

Always earthy, his brain stocked with parables and folk proverbs from his peasant origins, Khrushchev has compared American capitalism—in New Delhi on February 12, 1960, for instance—with a "limping horse," whereas "our socialist steed is full of energy." For some years American capitalism has been a high-powered automobile full of gasoline, but the driver has lolled along the magnificent parkways, stopping often to eat hamburgers. The Soviet steed has sped along pulling heavy loads of steel, coal, lathes, and luniks but not many shoes or women's dresses. "To catch up and then surpass America" is an old slogan coined by Stalin and used, with more justification, today. Soviet citizens, gradually immunized to propaganda, have been heard to say, "When you catch up with America let me off and go on without me."

It is unfair to blame Khrushchev for painting the United States in black colors. He cannot tell his people that it would never have occurred to President Eisenhower to ask factory employees in Chicago (or to President de Gaulle to ask workers in Marseilles) whether they really had milk and to congratulate them on an adequate supply of bread. The twelve Soviet authors of *Face to Face with America* are bound by their social commitments to characterize the United States pityingly as "a complicated and contradictory country where the overwhelming majority of the people remain imprisoned by the myth of the superiority of the capitalist way of life." Khrushchev himself, at the end of the thirteen days' visit described in that book, proclaimed that "the holiest of holy, the best that man can create is the socialist society, the communist system." He sees an unvaried, unmixed world. "My conviction is," Khrushchev told newsmen in Moscow on May 11, 1960, at the exhibit of the U.S. U-2 airplane shot down over Soviet territory, "that all roads lead to communism. What else can they lead to?" All roads? Some might lead to individual freedom, decency, peace, and a higher standard of living. Some might lead to the British system, or the Swedish system, or the American system, or the Indian system, or the Yugoslav system. He should ask his people to choose.

A Soviet leader must, of necessity, add propagandistic generalizations and theoretical abstractions to Russia's meager material achievements. "The thing to be borne in mind," Khrushchev insists, "is the noble aims of communism. Under capitalism, man is to man a wolf." This recalls an anecdote a Soviet citizen told in Moscow in 1956: "Capitalism is the exploitation of man by man. Communism is just the reverse." Khrushchev has apparently forgotten his secret speech of February 25, 1956. For twenty-five years Stalin was a wolf to millions of men. Things are better now, but the Soviet state is still an untamed wolf devouring a tremendous percentage of the national income and subtracting it from the people's well-being. The real choice is between the gray capitalist wolf, chained, checked, and balanced by government regulations, trade unions, civil liberties, noncapitalist parties, etc., and the red wolf over which the citizenry has no control.

Part of the high cost of the Soviet system is due to its inefficiency. Bureaucracy tends to corrupt and absolute bureaucracy corrupts absolutely. This is true in Soviet industry and farming. Khrushchev has endeavored to lift the heavy hand of the bureaucrat from village collectives by introducing personal peasant incentive, but the state still owns and manages them, and the state is run by bureaucrats.

Another part of the high cost of the Soviet system is due to its foreign policy. Khrushchev devotes an ever-increasing segment of his public addresses to international affairs. He must realize that the tension with the West and the problems created by Russia's domination of her satellites increase the national armaments budget and reduce the Soviet standard of living. This produces a Kremlin cancer. Khrushchev's proposed cure is slogans: "peaceful coexistence"; "end the cold war"; "total disarmament." He does not suggest friendship. When M. Groussard of *Le Figaro* informed the Soviet Chairman that he had communist friends and "the fact that they are communists, whereas I am not, does not weaken our friendship," Khrushchev commented, "I have different views on that matter. Friendship is real and strong when people see eye to eye on developments, history, and life. If you do not share the philosophy of the communist party . . . it would be hard for you to have deep friendship as we understand it." Instead of friendship and co-operation, Moscow advocates relaxation of tensions: the Soviet Union, says Khrushchev, views the summit conference "as a step toward relieving international tensions." Yet on the eve of that conference he increased tensions by attempting to undermine the western position in Berlin.

Khrushchev's foreign policy is an "on the one hand and on the other hand" amalgam. On the one hand (May 24, 1958), he proposed that the West "try the way of partial disarmament." On the other hand, at the United Nations in September 1959, he and, in 1960 at Geneva, his diplomats stubbornly demanded total disarmament in four years. On the one hand (June 11, 1958) Khrushchev affirmed that the Soviet Union "continues to advocate restoration of the national unity of the German people." Moreover (July 11, 1958), "Among these questions is the reunification of Germany. The western powers insist that the summit conference should take up this internal affair of the German people. It is perfectly clear, however, that this question is an internal matter for the German people and does not come within the competence of an international conference. To put forward this question for the conference agenda is to wreck the calling of such a conference."

To this Khrushchev statement the western powers might very well reply, "Good. Since the reunification of Germany is not the business of other countries, we will not discuss it but merely recommend to the West and East German governments that they set up a commission to deal with the matter. In the meantime, of course, summit conferences should not discuss Berlin, for if Germany is reunified there will be no Berlin problem."

It is not for me to prompt Khrushchev or to predict his reaction to such a western gambit. But whereas he states, on the one hand, that he favors German unity and would leave the matter to Germans only, on the other hand, he declares (June 11, 1958) that "the Soviet Union is ready to help the German people actively in creating a single peaceful and democratic Germany"—read, a single communist Germany—"and to support such proposals as the creation of a confederation of the two German states." Furthermore (July 8, 1958), "we believe that if today it is only the German Democratic Republic that is socialist, the time will come when all Germany will follow the socialist path." Finally (July 9, 1958), "Herr Adenauer and his colleagues . . . want to . . . make us exert pressure on the government of the German Democratic Republic so that it will agree to reunification at the price of abolishing the G.D.R. . . . If any leader in the Soviet Union were so much as to think that way, people in our country and our party would say that such a leader be placed in a lunatic asylum and have his head examined." Is Khrushchev for German reunification? At a banquet in his honor in Washington, D.C., on September 24, 1959, Khrushchev said, "If we will find a common language on questions of disarmament, if we will have a peace treaty with both German governments—that means we will see that you want to live in peace. If not—it means you want war." A peace treaty "with both German governments": in other words, Khrushchev wants a divided Germany.

On the one hand, coexistence. On the other hand (July 9, 1958), "capitalism and socialism are antagonistic social systems." On the one hand (July 9, 1958), "We say, it is necessary, as the diplomats put it, to recognize the status quo."

On the other hand, drive the West from West Berlin, disrupt NATO, and foster communism in all continents.

Stalin's face was grim but clear; Khrushchev's is smiling and puzzling. Stalin, the monolith, decided and acted. Khrushchev maneuvers to satisfy diverse forces within and mystify the adversary abroad. In coping with divisions inside the communist bloc he cleverly seeks to divide the western bloc.

Under Stalin there were no politics. Politics are the struggle for power. Stalin held all the power and the only struggle was to keep out of his big black executioner's book. Today, however, Russia is a political country. Not only is Khrushchev's domestic-political power, great though it be, less than Stalin's; the rise in education and the slightly increased independence of sections of the upper class, as well as the growing demand of the toiling masses for a larger flow of better-quality goods, has tended to diminish the rigors of totalitarianism. But the totalitarian needs of the empire and the desire of men who have power to keep it create a contrary tendency. Khrushchev is well-equipped to ride these two horses. For he is a combination of inborn temperament and the restraint he had to learn under Stalin's brutal school. He therefore blows hot and cold, alternates toughness with softness, is first firm then folksy, and at all times, both at home and abroad, plays the ham actor on tour. In some ways he is a wiser and wilier opponent than Stalin. In domestic affairs Stalin's chief weapon was the revolver, in foreign affairs the bludgeon. Khrushchev, accustomed to finer instruments inside, wields them outside as well and leaves his opposite numbers agape at the fancy footwork and fantastic fencing. He always retains the initiative because he knows the West will not go to war. He can, accordingly, create an international crisis when there is something to be gained thereby and relax it when it becomes too dangerous. The answer to Stalin's foreign strategy was obvious: the West checked postwar Soviet aggression by the Marshall Plan and NATO. To check Khrushchev NATO needs to become more than a military defense pact. It must be the foundation of an integrated Europe.

Stalin consistently opposed measures like the Marshall Plan which conduced to the unity of Europe. In this, Khrushchev is his heir. Unity spells greater prosperity and strength, and neither suits Moscow. More than that, unity through internationalism exposes the retrograde nationalism which Russia practices and preaches.

The Khrushchev era brought ferment, reform, and revision to Russia. It is a somewhat unpredictable, indeed contradictory, period. The Soviet forces of progress have to contend with the forces of conservatism and communist power lust. Economic necessity requires an accommodation between the regime and the individual and between the country and the world. Khrushchev has facilitated yet impeded this adjustment. He allows partial relaxation and talks coexistence. But the dictator and the many thousands of little dictators who populate the Soviet administration have a vested interest in perpetuating their positions. Long practice creates habits of action and thought in rulers and ruled that defy change especially when the system produces some desired results. This survival urge of dictatorship finds a prop in Soviet imperialism. If Russia were a democracy, Eastern Europe would today be experiencing the same process of liberation from colonialism which overtook Asia in the 1940's and Africa in the 1950's and 1960's. The collapse of the dictatorship would hasten the end of empire just as the end of empire would accelerate the death of the dictatorship.

Situated between Red China and more-or-less democratic Europe, the Soviet Union feels the pull of both. After the Second World War Stalin tried to expand into Central and

Western Europe, not merely for nationalist-imperialist reasons. He regarded a free Europe on his western flank as a menace to the dictatorship. He wanted communist-satellite buffers not against European military strength, which was nil and might have remained negligible but for his pressure; he wanted them as a cordon sanitaire against freedom. Stalin's ideal was a chaotic Europe and a chaotic China. Khrushchev's Russia faces a different kind of Europe and a different kind of China. Both are a problem to her. Khrushchev accordingly swings, pendulum-like, between coexistence with the West and co-ordination with China, meanwhile taking refuge in incomplete isolation buttressed by national arrogance and motivated by social fears for the dictatorship. Here the outside world has a role to play. A fully democratic West would crack the Chinese wall of Russian totalitarianism. A united, fully democratic Europe could help shape the fate of the Soviet Union.

## chapter 6

# The Creative Peninsula

EUROPE, the mother of wars, the mother of America, the mother of culture, seemed doomed after the Second World War. World power has been polarized toward the Soviet Union and the United States, leaving Europe as deflated politically as it was militarily, physically, and economically. Interest centered on emergent Asia and rumbling Africa. Europe looked like a shriveled old arthritic peninsula hanging limp from the bloated body of Asia.

In 1945 millions of Europeans lacked adequate food and housing and many more millions were unemployed. Jagged, blackened ruins faced whole cities on waking up and going to bed. Rubble filled the streets. Hope had collapsed.

Between 1914 and 1918, almost all destruction was confined to the battlefields and shipping. Between 1939 and 1945, hundreds of cities and thousands of industrial installations suffered withering damage. In the First World War the military casualties were enormous, the civilian victims few. In the second war millions of noncombatant men, women, and children died in air raids, in concentration camps, in gas ovens, and of starvation. Humanitarians and economists predicted that it would be a generation before Europe could crawl out from under the debris of the worst holocaust in the history of man.

Europe's recovery has exceeded all expectations in speed, extent, and solidity. Europe this side of the Soviet bloc is the most prosperous area of its size and population on the earth. Nineteen countries, counting approximately 400 million inhabitants, produce more and consume more than Russia plus her satellites and have richer trained manpower resources and potentially bigger military power than the Soviet Union.

In the middle of the nineteenth century Marx and Macaulay, one a radical revolutionist, the other a conservative lord, despaired of prosperity and counseled dictatorship. The future of Europe looked as grim as its slums. Since then man has learned the secrets of production and distribution. Even the costliest of conflicts reversed the upward economic climb for a short time only. Materially, Europe is better off than ever.

"In the highly developed countries," Gunnar Myrdal, Swedish economist, notes in his book *Rich Lands and Poor* (1957), "all indices point steadily upward . . . business slumps and depressions and even severe setbacks due to wars appear only as short-term waverings of the firmly rising long-term trend." This has been Europe's experience. Asia, Africa, and Latin America would benefit by studying it. The startling recovery of Europe in so short a time after so grievous a war is a lesson in the significance of engineering know-how, in the value of a skilled, industrious working class, in the importance of administrative capacity and stable government, and in the effectiveness of international economic co-operation when properly handled. The Marshall Plan primed the European pump. But European ingenuity, organization, and experience are responsible for the high level of progress achieved and maintained.

The act of Congress which authorized U.S. financing of the Marshall Plan stressed "the advantages which the United States has enjoyed through the existence of a large domestic market without trade barriers," and the amended act of

April, 1949, stated concisely that it is "the policy of the people of the United States to encourage the unification of Europe."

The United States wants to see a new Europe: united, strong, self-reliant, and not dependent on outside material or military assistance. Already most European nations do not need and do not receive U.S. economic help. Someday America's part in European co-ordinated defense arrangements may taper off to long-distance support. The key to the future of Europe is unity.

The unification of Western, Northern, and Southern Europe will be a slow, zigzagging process. But the process has commenced, and partial success has been achieved. This is the most creative phenomenon in world affairs. For it represents a new stage in the development of human society. Civilization witnessed the rise of city-states, of counties and principalities, and then of nation-states. Now Europe has conceived the international state. Europe is attempting to graduate from nationalism into internationalism.

Nationalism served useful cultural, economic, and political purposes. It also fostered many wars and ugly passions. It is a phase, an illness one might say, through which every people must pass. The sooner countries win national independence the sooner will they evolve to the higher form of internationalism.

The eclipse of western empires in Asia and Africa serves as the main propellent toward European internationalism. Imperialism—or export nationalism—is incompatible with internationalism. So long as European powers were intent on holding, reinforcing, and extending their colonial realms there was bound to be rivalry and conflict. Today Asia and most of Africa are no longer objects of foreign domination. Opportunities for territorial expansion in Europe have fortunately dwindled to zero. No combination of powers can wrest Russia's satellites from her by force. And in the unlikely event of a war between France and Germany or Germany and England the beneficiary would be the Soviet Union.

The folly of war and the passing of empire have ushered in Europe's new internationalist era. The world supremacy of Russia and America and the looming figure of China make competition within Europe grotesque. This radical political change marches hand in hand with sentiment. Two emotional shifts of transcendent importance have taken place: the closing of the gulf between France and Germany and the narrowing of the Channel between England and Europe.

Khrushchev pranced through France in 1960 attempting to stir ancient hatred by recalling the ravages of three German invasions in seventy years. His poison campaign failed to move the French people. Nobody took his bait of a Russo-French combination against Germany. France and Russia, de Gaulle told him, were allies "when, twice in the course of this century, their continent found itself menaced by an ambition without measure which has since then disappeared." Germany's ambition had disappeared; Russia's had appeared. The unlikelihood of a fourth German invasion made nonsense of further hate. Hatred was the effect of previous wars and preparation for another. The elimination of a possible war between France and Germany tends to extinguish the hate. President de Gaulle emphasized Europe's great transformation in an address to the British Houses of Parliament on April 7, 1960. He hoped, he said, that the present peace "shall not widen division or poison wounds, including those suffered by the German people who were yesterday our enemies but who today are a vital part of the West and our common ally." At every official, social, economic, and professional level in France and Germany there is a conscious endeavor to close the blood book of the past.

On November 28, 1959, Sydney Gruson reported from Bonn to the *New York Times* about a French physician who had spent four years in a nazi concentration camp. Thereafter he refused to visit Germany. But in 1959 he did so. A friend asked why. "I thought it was time to come," the doctor replied, "when my son said to me, 'You know, father, so long as there are people who think as you do there will always be wars between us and the Germans.'"

The crimes committed by nazi Germany before and during the war were so monstrous that not-forgiving leaves only one alternative: to ostracize. Ostracism would breed the very evils Europe and the world must avoid.

Prime Minister David Ben-Gurion talked for two hours with Adenauer in New York on March 14, 1960, after which the Jewish leader said, "I was glad to meet Chancellor Adenauer. My people cannot forget its past, but we remember the past not in order to brood upon it but in order that it shall never recur. I said in the Knesset [Israeli parliament] last summer that the Germany of today is not the Germany of yesterday. After having met the Chancellor I am sure the judgment was correct." The nazi slaughter of six million Jews is a living, continuing tragedy that rules out Jewish diplomatic doubletalk. The man of Jerusalem spoke from his heart. He did not forget. He was constructive. Faith in human corrigibility is therapeutic. Stubborn, static rejection is understandable as an emotion. As politics it is futile, barren, and harmful.

In the summer of 1960 thirty West German students, aged fifteen to eighteen, members of the World Peace Service, settled in the Greek village of Servia, destroyed with wanton cruelty by Hitler's army. The teenagers had volunteered to stay a year and build eight hundred houses, a reservoir, and a new irrigation system. This is the type of penance that cures. It spreads the truth at home and erects a bridge abroad.

The British people too have many reasons for resenting Germans. But self-interest is on the side of moderation. Sir Ivone Kirkpatrick, England's high commissioner in Germany after the Second World War and subsequently permanent undersecretary of the Foreign Office, wrote in the London *Times* of August 3, 1960: "It is of course understandable that the experience of two world wars should have generated emotion, but in the present state of the world indulgence in prejudice and emotion is a luxury we cannot afford; and if we have regard to our safety we should base our policy on rational thinking."

"It's rather frightening to find that we of all people should be prisoners of our past," said a British ambassador quoted by Drew Middleton in the *New York Times* of April 5, 1960. "We've got to stop this nonsense about the Germans." Middleton noted that "Eight other members of NATO, occupied by the Germans in World War II, find it easy to forgive if not to forget."

The British attitude toward Germans has changed less than the French, but it has changed and is changing. An even greater accelerator of European unity is the shrinking of the English Channel. Psychologically the English Channel used to be as wide as the Atlantic Ocean. "Storm over Channel, Continent Isolated" was the way a famous London paper headlined its news. The "beastly" weather isolated the Continent, not England. When Britons crossed the Channel they were "going to Europe." They were not of Europe. The Channel made their country a mental island. Today, however, the island is visibly approaching the mainland. Mind alters geography.

In welcoming General de Gaulle to her country in April,

1960, Queen Elizabeth emphasized that the English Channel must not form a psychological barrier to "real understanding between Britain and France, between Britain and the other countries of Western Europe." These words represent a policy as well as a hope.

The project of a tunnel under the Channel or a bridge over it is both a symbol and a practical demonstration of Europe's irrepressible urge toward integration. The idea of a sub-Channel tunnel was broached to Napoleon in 1802. A French engineer named Thome de Gamond (1807-1875) made the first geological explorations and, having convinced himself that a tunnel was feasible, came to England and was presented to Queen Victoria and Prince Albert. Victoria, who suffered from seasickness, approved the idea. "You may tell the French engineer," she instructed the British minister in Paris, "that if he can accomplish it, I will give my blessing in my own name and in the name of all the ladies of England." In 1870 the British and French governments exchanged notes on the question of the tunnel. The Franco-Prussian War interrupted these negotiations, but in June, 1872, the British government informed France that it agreed in principle to the tunnel. That same year the first Channel Tunnel Company was formed, and the borings commenced in 1881. The British got as far as one mile out to sea from the foot of Shakespeare Cliff, Dover. The co-operating French firm reached a point under the Channel 1½ miles from Sangatte, near Calais. The British military authorities, however, fearing an invasion from the Continent via the tunnel (although arrangements had been envisaged for quick flooding in the event of war), persuaded their government to interdict further operations.

John Bright, the British freetrader, wrote in 1887: "Our people, or many of them, are very silly about matters concerning foreigners. The invention of steamships was infinitely more dangerous to us than the tunnel or a dozen tunnels." In the era of jet planes, mass parachute drops, and rockets, the tunnel as a military menace is comic. What Soviet general, having conquered France, would, instead of first crippling Britain with atomic and hydrogen missiles, send his army into a 36-mile tunnel, whose complicated ventilation system could be stopped and which could easily be blocked? Or the soldiers might be allowed to emerge on the British side into a murderous rain of shells and bullets. Mr. Harold Macmillan said on February 16, 1955, while minister of defense, that strategic objections to the tunnel no longer existed. The engineering and financial obstacles, all agree, can be overcome. Now the question is no longer, Tunnel, yes or no? but Tunnel or bridge? The bridge would be 21 miles long, cost $560 million (200 million pounds sterling), and take five years to erect. Anyone with imagination can see, before the end of the twentieth century, a tunnel and a bridge carrying goods and people and linking the British mind to the Continent and the Continent to Britain. At the opposite end of the Continent, a bridge across the Bosporus is to connect Asia with Europe. Before long, continents will be a geography-book fiction.

As technology revolutionizes man's concepts of speed, space, and time, politics and economics must keep in step or die of obsolescence. The real revolution of our age is not communism—that is just the old dressed in prison garb on an express train—but jet propulsion, nuclear energy, and planetary navigation. These make national barriers look rather silly. Science is an agent of internationalism.

We are the witnesses of a remarkable reversal of roles in world affairs. The communists were the original political internationalists and proponents of science as against religion. Today the Soviets use science as an implement but their outlook is not scientific. Having dethroned God, they filled a pantheon with many gods propped up by dogma. Doubt was anathema and false prophecy preferred to hard facts. Under the same reactionary influence they became nationalists at home and imperialists abroad. The West, on the contrary, is slowly replacing obscurantism with science and nationalism with internationalism. Europe, encouraged by the United States, leads the way to its own unity. Stalin was and Khrushchev is a great help. Europe felt threatened and drew closer together. But even if the problems of waging and preventing war did not exist, there would still be an urgent need to end the fragmentation of Europe. Hence the interesting nature of NATO (North Atlantic Treaty Organization) which, conceived as a military alliance, has, since its inauguration in 1949, become much more.

Though called "North Atlantic," NATO stretches from Turkey's Black Sea to Greece's Aegean, to Italy's Adriatic, to France's Mediterranean, to Britain's and Holland's North Sea, to Norway's Arctic Ocean, to Canada's Hudson Bay, to the Pacific coast of the United States. This fifteen-nation defense entente manifests many shortcomings. It has not attained its targets in manpower and equipment and remains too dependent on the United States. Most member countries spend more on alcohol, tobacco, fancy automobiles, and gadgets than on NATO. Nations, not unnaturally, finance military preparedness reluctantly, material progress avidly. Nevertheless, NATO has collected a formidable force to face the first phase of a Soviet attack. NATO's armed might consists of those fractions of member armies, navies, and airfleets which the fifteen governments consent to place at its disposal. It is thus a frame or cadre which could be filled in and expanded endlessly in case of crisis.

The originality of NATO lies in its not being a mere coalition, a mere concert of countries pledged by treaty to bring their separate military establishments to bear on an aggressor. NATO, in peacetime, integrates national contingents into a single standing international defense force with a view to war prevention and, if necessary, war waging. Its design is novel in that member states allow their military units to be commanded by nonnationals. In 1950, the second year of its existence, NATO decided to establish a Supreme Headquarters, Allied Powers Europe (SHAPE), and in 1951 General Dwight D. Eisenhower was named Supreme Commander. His successors were U.S. Generals Albert M. Gruenther and Lauris Norstad. The deputy supreme commander in 1959 was an Englishman, General Sir Richard N. Gale, and in 1960 his countryman, General Sir Hugh Stockwell. Lord Ismay of Britain retired as General Secretary of NATO in 1957, to be replaced by Paul-Henri Spaak, a Belgian, a civilian, and a socialist. An American commands NATO's North Atlantic fleet; an Englishman is his assistant. In 1957 West German General Hans Speidel was appointed commander in chief of NATO's land forces. Lieutenant General Aldo Rossi of Italy became commander of NATO's armies in Southern Europe in 1958. In 1960 French General Maurice Challe took over command of NATO's Central European sector.

Year by year NATO has been building up an infrastructure of connecting tissue which, though essentially military, has economic connotations and political consequences. For instance, NATO recently completed and put in use a 3,000-mile underground pipeline with appropriate tanks capable of storing one million tons of fuel for jet and propellor planes stationed on 160 NATO airfields. The pipeline, laid in Belgium, France, Germany, Holland, and Luxembourg, paid for—$200 million—by the fifteen members, is available to all of them. It is international in the additional sense

that no taxes or customs duties are levied on the liquid that
passes through it. Separate NATO pipelines operate in
Greece, Turkey, Denmark, Norway, and Italy.

Another military-economic NATO enterprise: After considerable study, NATO chose the French turboprop Breguet
1150, renamed "Atlantic," for antisubmarine patrol purposes. France, Germany, Holland, and Belgium manufacture
parts of the plane; Britain supplies the Rolls-Royce engines;
the United States supplies much of the electronic equipment
and some of the money.

NATO tends to expand its functions. The foreign ministers of the fifteen member states meet frequently to discuss
specific and broad political questions. Every NATO country
accredits a permanent civilian ambassador to SHAPE in
Paris. Annually a conference of members of parliament of
the NATO nations convenes to debate issues confronting
the alliance. Many of the legislators are influential in their
parties and though their resolutions are not binding they
carry weight. This conference may be the prototype of a
real European parliament. Addressing its session in Washington on November 19, 1959, Paul-Henri Spaak said it was
time "to revise and expand" NATO to include economic
commitments to Asia and Africa. Canada's Prime Minister
John Diefenbaker has asked NATO to open a "food bank"
for emergencies. Because world conditions are ripe for internationalism, NATO, hastily assembled in 1949 to deter Soviet aggression, has grown into something beyond the dreams
of its fathers, has, indeed, begun to grow international limbs
and brains.

It would be a miracle if NATO were without flaws.
Though many recognize that the first law of politics, economics, security, friendship, and love is interdependence,
the old illness of illusory national self-interest, which in this
age is self-defeating, plagues the new body of NATO. De

Gaulle has been the worst offender. Some contend that France is less nationalistic than her president and that obeisances to his dreams of national grandeur and glory are the price paid to bring this political recluse out of retirement into service. Maybe. The fact remains that with the bulk of her military manpower committed to a wasteful war in Algeria, France has insisted on a role in NATO out of all relation to her contribution to the organization. His impersonal megalomania thwarted, de Gaulle in 1959 denied NATO the right to stockpile nuclear weapons on French soil, removed the French Mediterranean fleet from NATO control, and refused to participate in the united air defense of continental Europe. As a result, more than two hundred American fighter-bombers based on French airfields had to be shifted to England and Germany. De Gaulle behaved in consonance with his principle of "co-operation, not co-ordination," a rejection, in effect, of NATO's basic philosophy and a departure from internationalism. On the other hand, he was irate when the United States did not support his stand on Algeria in the UN debate. But an alliance forged to impede Soviet imperialism cannot consistently support imperialism in its own ranks. Algeria is an obstacle to Europe's unification. De Gaulle, who knows Europe needs unity and has contributed measurably to that unity, also obstructs it—and France's role in Africa—by delaying a solution in Algeria. De Gaulle's precise mind turns him to the future. His emotions enslave him to the past.

But nobody has a monopoly of minuses or pluses. De Gaulle's firmness probably blocked the blow Khrushchev aimed in 1959-1960 at West Berlin, the key to NATO's survival. There is reason to believe, and no published documents to prove, that during the September, 1959, secret Camp David talks President Eisenhower, employing the kind of imprecise statement for which his press conferences have become famous, gave Chairman Khrushchev the impression of an American readiness to alter "the abnormal situation" of West Berlin in a manner congenial to Soviet designs on the exposed city. Thereupon, the "Spirit of Camp David" was hailed from a thousand communist microphones. Subsequently, however, General de Gaulle told Khrushchev, with Adenauer's blessing, that the western powers would not weaken West Berlin through a summit conference compromise. When Secretary of State Herter and Undersecretary Dillon then made speeches in line with de Gaulle's intransigence, Khrushchev had no further use for the May summit conference and used the convenient coincidence of the U-2 episode to break up the heads-of-nation meeting.

No democratic alliance can be a bed of roses. It is more like a Procrustean bed of nails on which all members refuse to lie down simultaneously. The remarkable thing is not that NATO has encountered trouble but that it works at all. It has worked.

One would expect, and one actually finds, smoother progress toward internationalism in the economic realm, for trade between countries is ancient history, and modern industry needs raw materials, patents, markets, and finances not always available within national frontiers.

On March 19, 1951, delegates from France, Italy, Germany, and Benelux (Belgium, Netherlands, Luxembourg) signed a fifty-year treaty establishing the Coal and Steel Community with a view to eliminating national restrictions on commerce in coal and steel, standardizing production, and redirecting workers. It was assumed that some weak companies would founder in consequence of the abolition of frontiers. Private interests might suffer. The citizens of the Community were sure to benefit.

The Community set up a High Authority as its chief executive body with instructions to oppose coal and steel cartels that fixed prices, controlled markets, and monopolized raw materials. The Community also created a special council of cabinet ministers of the six nations, a Community Assembly consisting of members of parliament of the six countries which would meet annually, and a Court of Justice of seven judges to rule on treaty violations.

The Coal and Steel Community was the brain child of Robert Schuman, French foreign minister. Jean Monnet of France conducted most of the negotiations. The foreign ministers of the six participating nations gave the treaty its final form, and John J. McCloy, then American high commissioner in Germany, lent his influence and experience to the successful conclusion of the complicated give-and-take that preceded the birth of the organization. The Community officially came to life on February 10, 1953, after the six parliaments had ratified the treaty.

When Monnet, the French government's leading economist, took office as president of the High Authority, he said the Community was "an important step toward the eventual unification of Europe which is its only salvation." Secretary of State Dean Acheson called the Community "the first major step toward the unification of Europe."

Economic in practice, the Coal and Steel Community is thus political in concept. It could not be otherwise. Politics are involved the moment nations agree to lower or efface national frontiers for persons or commodities.

The Parliamentary Assembly of the Coal and Steel Community held its last annual session in Strasbourg on February 28, 1958, and was absorbed into the European Parliamentary Assembly of the new European Economic Community, or Common Market, and of the European Atomic Energy Community, or Euratom. The Common Market and Euratom embrace the same six countries—France, Germany, Italy, and Benelux. As constituted by the Rome treaty of

March 25, 1957, both bodies are intergovernmental and operate under a Council of Ministers recruited from high officials of the several nations. In this case, again, an economic enterprise was found to require an international political superstructure.

The Common Market proposes to abolish all tariffs and customs between the member states and to co-ordinate all their economic activities. The many become one for industry, finance, and trade—an economic United States. The effect would be to standardize, to rationalize, and to eliminate duplication and the waste of labor, time, and materials. This is the plan. Fulfillment, its authors claim, requires twelve to fifteen years.

Next to the United States of America, the Six, as the Common Market is called, are the biggest producer-consumer in the world. This gives them tremendous power. This also frightens nonmembers. For the Six will not merely lower and ultimately scrap tariff barriers; they will erect a tariff barrier around the entire territory against outsiders. England and other countries saw this as a threat: they would be excluded, in whole or part, from a very rich market. Under British leadership, accordingly, the European Free Trade Area was organized consisting of the United Kingdom, Denmark, Sweden, Norway, Austria, Switzerland, and Portugal, known as the Seven. They did not intend to co-ordinate their economies after the manner of the Six. They proposed to deal with tariff duties only.

The Seven were conceived as a protective association against the effects of the unification of the Six—a platform for negotiation. In fact, at the instance of Austria, Denmark, and Switzerland, according to Austrian Foreign Minister Bruno Kreisky, in the *New Leader* of April 25, 1960, the preamble of the European Free Trade Association's original

Stockholm Agreement gives its aim as "European-wide integration." Already Great Britain, the bastion of the Seven, is moving toward the Six. When the Coal and Steel Community was proposed, the British Foreign Secretary Ernest Bevin, the blunt Labour leader and nationalist, rejected it. "This Pandora's box," he said, using a startling mixture of metaphors, "is full of Trojan horses." Yet since then the Conservative government has offered to join the Coal and Steel Community and Euratom, and powerful voices in England are insisting that the United Kingdom join the European Common Market. "What will happen," if it stays out, according to Alan Day's BBC address (*The Listener,* July 7, 1960) "will be a steady decline in Britain's influence in the world: our economy will be less dynamic than it would be if we joined the Six." British civil servants, politicians, and political writers have noted a mounting indifference of the Six to what England does. Andrew Shonfield, the economic editor of the influential London *Observer,* therefore warns that "the main point which the Government has to understand is that if it is to get into the Common Market now, it must want to do so hard enough to kick down the door." He sees "the risk of being rebuffed" but suggests that Britain must demand "her birthright as a European nation."

"Nothing can exempt us for long from what is happening in Europe," writes J. T. Beresford, a farmer and specialist on farm problems, in the London *Times* agricultural supplement of July 5, 1960. "There is no exemption from the future. We have now to meet the situation as we find it. As a nation we have lost our big chance of leadership in Europe." This may be true because the day of leader nations is gone—even for the United States. England can, however, still be a partner. As long ago as August 17, 1957, the London *Economist* said, "Britain's economic and political future does lie more and more with Europe," and on March 5, 1960, "Resisting unification of Europe would be tantamount to flying in the face of the forces of salutary change."

Nevertheless, Englishmen did resist. Moscow, having vainly courted France, might, some argued, be more successful with an offer to reunify Germany on condition that she become a totalitarian ally of Russia. Irrespective of the cogency of this proposition—and it does not seem to reflect reality—the certain disaster for the West if it were true would dictate a policy of prevention through tighter unity. ". . . our policy," Sir Ivone Kirkpatrick wrote in his *Times* article, "must be firmly directed towards helping . . . to anchor Germany in the western block. We should be in a better position to do this if we were more closely associated with Europe." West Germany and France and Italy, Britons have declared, are not as democratic or law-abiding as England. Great Britain is undoubtedly the most democratic of the big powers and the equal in democracy of the best of the small states—say Switzerland. But the Frenchman's daily way of life is the essence of freedom, no matter what his government has done so far. German democracy, all its inadequacies notwithstanding, has a stability it never had between the two wars. If nazism was the ugly offspring of six million unemployed and nationalistic aggressiveness, its chances of revival are nil. Conscious of her bad past, West Germany, when she joined the Western European Union in 1954, voluntarily renounced the manufacture of large weapons like tanks and bombers and of atomic, chemical, and bacteriological instruments of death. As a member of NATO, with military depots, airfields, training grounds, and staff headquarters in Belgium, Holland, France, and Great Britain, and with foreign NATO troops on her soil, West Germany is less likely to cause international trouble and more likely to follow her partners toward democracy than if she were denounced and cold-shouldered into resentment. The way to make a friend is to be a friend. The wise welcome partial atonement instead of waiting for total reformation. The final British contention that Britain cannot merge with the European economy while merged with the Commonwealth is weak. Nobody has demonstrated the fiscal and commercial incompatibility of belonging to both. The Commonwealth itself and the Common Market Six have made numerous economic adjustments and are capable of more.

High officials of the Six and the Seven predict that England will join the Six by 1962. She is moving over. Unwittingly, de Gaulle helped. So long as there was a hope of converting the Common Market Six from an economic organization into a European political federation, West Germany, Belgium, Holland, Italy, and Luxembourg made one concession after the other to de Gaulle's appetite for leadership. To achieve this leadership, Great Britain, with her power and political sagacity, had to be kept out of the Six. The British themselves felt reluctant to enter a political federation. But the moment President de Gaulle clearly indicated, in private talks with Adenauer and then in his September 6, 1960 press conference, that he wanted no federal union, that all he wanted was French predominance in Europe and a special role for France in Africa, France's five partners in the Six saw no further reason to feed de Gaulle's hunger for glory and every reason to bring Great Britain into the Common Market. Moreover, now that the Common Market had, at least temporarily, lost its political-federation overtones, British aversion to it ebbed.

The results were: a notable strengthening of Anglo-German relations and added British support for Adenauer's foreign policy; growing British sympathy for the Common Market; and a weakening of France's position in Europe and Africa. By being an overzealous nationalist, de Gaulle had damaged the national interests of France. Someday, he and the French or the French without him will have to reverse his policy and favor a European federal union in which France plays a part commensurate with her contribution. Presumably, also, British membership in the Common Market, the Coal and Steel Community, and Euratom, could, in time, diminish England's traditional antagonism to political intimacy with foreign nations.

The obstacles to European union are infinite in number. The trend, nevertheless, is irresistible and irreversible. All the news about consultations, recriminations, door-banging, and fist-shaking are but part of the zigzagging progress toward integration. No serious person expects the early rise of a United States of Europe in which the nations of today become states under a federal government as in the United States of America. The nations will keep their identity and individuality for years. Love of country and locality remains. But nationalism, Europe realizes, is no longer an adequate service to nations. It is a barrier in a world that needs bridges. The nations of Europe with the greatest experience in nationalism now know its shortcomings and are striving to marry it to internationalism.

The Six and the Seven together will exert a strong pull on Greece, Turkey, Ireland, Iceland, Spain, and Finland, conceivably even on Yugoslavia. This would close the long dark age of Europe's economic balkanization. But a united Europe need not be an exclusive club. The Mediterranean is only a ditch. If Holland is joined to Italy, why not to Tunisia too? Why not a Tunisian-Algerian-Moroccan federation linked with Europe? Far from being destructive of nationalism, such independence-in-interdependence would be the best guarantee of security and prosperity in a world where hurricanes rage.

European unity means more than NATO and the Common Market, more than military, economic, and political strength, infinitely more than a bulwark against communism. It can save England from isolation and from "apparent docile servility to Washington," in the words of a member of Parliament. It would save Germany from the doubts—partly responsible for the first and second world wars—whether she was of the West or the East. It could rescue Russia from mystic messianism and tear down the high wall that has shut her in for many centuries since the Tatar conquest and subsequent western invasions. European unity is not against Russia, it is for Russia. It would lift her out of the nineteenth century into the twentieth; she has always been late. European unity will create a free partnership for fruitful, life-giving co-operation with Asia, Africa, and Latin America.

## chapter 7

# The Vanity of Empire

LIFE is change. Every human being and every social system changes constantly. Intelligent persons know this and Marxists believe it. Marxism as a philosophy is based on dialectics, on the assumption of uninterrupted change. "The parasitism and decay of capitalism," Lenin wrote in 1916, ". . . are characteristic of its highest stage of development, that is imperialism." Therefore, "imperialism is the eve of the proletarian social revolution." Capitalism, being parasitic and decadent, would die; communism would succeed it. Lenin's reasoning was dialectic. It predicated capitalism's growth to a highest stage, its violent death, and the rise of a red heir. Thesis, antithesis, synthesis.

What a pity Lenin cannot see Holland today. He would discover that though Holland lost an empire she found a new lease on life. The process of change brought not death but health.

Scorning reform, judging all capitalist systems by Russia's, Lenin overlooked the reserves of recuperation and rejuvenation in western society. The example of Holland, and of England, suggests that imperialism is actually the companion of a low stage of capitalism, of capitalism in its unripe and hence predatory youth. The empires of Spain, Portugal, Holland, and England were founded not in their highest capitalist stage but in the sixteenth, seventeenth, and eighteenth centuries, in the age of feudalism and underdevelopment, or, at the latest, in capitalism's juvenile, mercantile stage. England and Holland used soldiers to conquer the colonies but sent trading companies to administer them. Only around the middle of the nineteenth century did imperialism begin to assume its final form: the imperial power took over from the trading association and installed a colonial government to control all the affairs of the colony. This step was dictated by fear that another country might seize the possession, fear of native unrest, and a desire to extract more raw material and food for the metropolitan's growing industry and population and bigger profits from investment and trade.

The case of the Dutch East Indies, today's Indonesia, shows the immaturity of capitalist imperialism as late as the second decade of the nineteenth century. During the Napoleonic Wars, France occupied Holland and the Dutch Indies. England, waging a global war with Bonaparte, ousted the French from the Indies and in 1811 sent Sir Thomas Stamford Raffles to govern them.

Raffles was a remarkable man, a revolutionary innovator, an enemy of slavery, a foe of feudalism. During his four-year rule of the Indies he introduced capitalist ownership of land, downgraded the native feudal princes, and planned to make the Indies a second India under permanent British sovereignty. He anticipated, he said, that the Indies would become a rich field for British capital investment.

Both as a social reformer and as an imperialist, however, Raffles was ahead of his time and of his home government. The British East India Company, despite its monopoly of trade with the Indies, had little interest in the colony because business during Raffles' four war years proved unprofitable. Nor did the British government wish to keep the Indies, chock-full of natural resources though they were. On August 13, 1814, at the Congress of Vienna convened to restore political order after Napoleon's volcanic adventures, Lord

Castlereagh, the British foreign secretary, returned Indonesia to Holland. The Dutch were also given Belgium and Luxembourg. England intended to reinforce Holland as a bulwark against French and Prussian conquest of the Low Countries whence they might threaten the British Isles. These arrangements in Europe seemed more important than empire in Asia.

Politics took precedence over economics—something a Marxist would not expect. But Lenin also misinterpreted the economic aspects of capitalism. In his 1916 *Imperialism* book, he declared that "the necessity of exporting capital arises from the fact that in a few countries capitalism has become 'over-ripe' and (owing to the backward state of agriculture and the impoverished state of the masses) capital cannot find 'profitable' investment."

This was true, but Lenin made the mistake of thinking it always would be. "Where," he asked in the same work, "except in the imagination of sentimental reformers are there any trusts capable of interesting themselves in the conditions of the masses instead of in the conquest of colonies?" Neglect of the masses at home and imperial conquest had an additional motivation. "The more capitalism is developed," Lenin wrote, "the more the need for raw materials is felt." Already, he pointed out, "there is a growing shortage of timber . . . of leather, and raw materials for the textile industry." No thought of plastics and other substitutes. He also spoke of "the exhaustion of the American oil wells." No thought of new oilfields in Texas, Oklahoma, California, and Kansas.

How dangerous it is to judge the future by the present and the past! How unwise to put limits on man's ingenuity and adjustability! How wrong even so great a leader and theoretician as Lenin could be!

Dialectics did not help Lenin. Like Khrushchev, who said in the United States that capitalism was no different today than in Marx's day, Lenin wanted to believe that in an ever-changing world capitalism would not change. He noted correctly that instead of building decent homes for human beings where stood England's grimy slums, instead of raising wages which would pay food, doctor, and dental bills, the capitalists were exporting large sums to the colonies and to the United States, Latin America, and elsewhere for the sake of bigger profits than cheap housing could yield. He failed to anticipate, however, that deepening democracy in the West and rising independence demands in the East would force capitalism to divest itself of its colonies. The yellow, brown, and black man would shed his imperial shackles, and after that, partly as a result of that, the white man would achieve a better material life at home. The very condition which led Lenin to his pessimistic prognosis about capitalism contained the potential of the system's regeneration. Excessive capital exports, he had found, were at the expense of the masses in capitalist nations. After the Second World War, when the domestic economy had first call on available capital, improvement set in for the masses and everybody.

Lenin seemed right in 1916, and in 1929 and 1939, but not in 1949, much less in 1959. Events have invalidated his theory. Somebody might have said to him what Goethe wrote in *Faust:*

> Grey, dear friend, is all theory,
> And green is life's golden tree.

Lenin himself quoted this in 1914, and on June 3, 1958, Khrushchev quoted it from Lenin, adding a comment that makes superfluous any further comment on Lenin's imperialism-is-the-highest-and-last-stage-of-capitalism theory. "Theoretical propositions which seemed infallible," Khrushchev declared, "were repeatedly put forward in the history of human society, but they did not stem from life itself and were not confirmed by practice. Such theoretical postulates soon died, without being of any benefit to mankind." Khrushchev, of course, did not apply this to Lenin's theory of imperialism. But it fits.

Theoreticians of the world, beware. Distill theory from the past and present if you know how to add a rich sprinkling of imagination. Otherwise, life's golden tree will dispel your gray visions of gloom just as the history of Western Europe has dispelled Lenin's. It is not true that democracy leads to imperialism and that imperialism ends in the destruction of democracy. The reverse is true. The expansion of democracy leads to the end of imperialism and then to the further expansion of democracy. Imperialism, in western countries as in Soviet Russia, has been and is the product of underdeveloped democracy and underdeveloped capitalism. Both are lifted to a higher plane when empire goes.

Holland is a classic example of welfare gains despite colonial losses. With 11 million inhabitants and practically no natural resources—even farmland has to be lifted out of the sea—Holland is better off now than when she ruled Indonesia. Next to the United States and the Soviet Union, Indonesia is the world's richest country in subsoil and agricultural wealth; it has petroleum, tin, coal, bauxite, manganese, copper, nickel, tea, coffee, sugar, rubber, copra, palm oil. And vast areas of this country of 90 million inhabitants remain unexplored. Forced to relinquish their Oriental treasure house, the Dutch roused themselves to a supreme effort of adaption to life without an empire. As in war, so in the crisis precipitated by the 1949 alienation of tropical Indonesia, the stubborn, frugal, hard-working North Sea nation refused to sit down by the ruins of a realm and weep; it remade itself. Gross national product mounted from 17.5 billion guilders in 1949 to 25 billion in 1955. In the same period imports doubled and exports more than doubled. In those seven fat years Holland invested 32,360,000,000 guilders in her economy, yet her people ate better, dressed better, built more homes, and bought more bicycles and automobiles. The eclipse of empire tapped new sources of human energy. Moreover, science stepped in when imperialism failed. At the town of Pernis in Holland, for instance, the Dutch have built a giant synthetic rubber plant which will supply all the rubber requirements of Holland and leave large quantities for export. The Dutch used to get their rubber from Indonesian plantations.

Great Britain has, since the Second World War, granted freedom to India, Pakistan, Burma, Ceylon, and Malaya in Asia and to several of her African possessions. Nevertheless, she was able, in the thirteen years after that costly conflict, to build three million family homes and introduce free medicine for all. This is not the capitalism Marx and Lenin knew when they lived in London.

England was richer and stronger than Holland and France. Since her empire had attained world proportions her people and some of her statesmen took a larger view and evolved a global policy. They foresaw the advantage of making peace with the inevitable instead of waiting to be overwhelmed by it. England may have learned this lesson from her mistakes in Ireland. The British knew what time it was; the hour of empire had struck. Realizing that Winston Churchill intended to hold the booty of the past, the British nation which loved him for his wartime leadership defeated him before even the war was ended and sent Clement R. Attlee to Ten Downing Street with a mandate, in effect, to liberate India. Since 1946, Labour and Conservative governments have negotiated with independence movements and retired from more and more colonies. Weaker nations, imprisoned by considerations of prestige and inspired by obsolete nationalistic notions, refused to yield to the modern temper. The Dutch, for example, fought for four years to keep Indonesia, only to be ousted in the end. India, consequently, co-operates with England within the Commonwealth whereas Holland and Indonesia are embittered, impassioned enemies. Paris created a community through which newly independent African states might continue their cultural, economic, and other ties with France. Yet the Algerian war ate at the vitals and morale of the nation.

Frenchmen say they do not want their country to become a big Switzerland. What makes France exciting is not her African jungles, mountains, deserts, plains, and casbahs. She is great because of the French Revolution, because of her philosophers, scientists, writers, painters, scholars, and cooks, because her people have genius and temperament, because Paris is magnificently elegant, because the French language is beautiful. The suppression of a prolonged colonial revolt adds nothing to the greatness of a nation or the glory of an army. It detracts from both.

In the past a liberated possession might be seized by another power. This is an unjustifiable apprehension today. No western nation is panting to expand or found an empire. History moves in the opposite direction. The Soviet Union might, to be sure, gain influence in a newly liberated state through communist subversion and government financial assistance, just as the United States might replace the former motherland as the source of investment capital, technological aid, and arms. By delaying independence the imperial power can only hasten such developments. Moreover, few colonies released from bondage have shown a wish to forge fresh chains for themselves. For every Asian and African newcomer that has joined an American-sponsored alliance ten remain sternly aloof. Soviet penetration frequently rings premature alarm bells. Where, as in Indonesia for instance, the communists seem to be gaining the upper hand, effective antibodies develop, usually in the shape of military nationalists.

The situation in all new states remains fluid, but if it does not warrant complacency neither does it warrant hysteria. The hand of the giver is often bitten, and Soviet successes with this or that Afro-Asian government can prove to be a temporary or Pyrrhic victory. The United States too might exercise caution. Americans are frequently unaware that their actions, though legal and helpful, may boomerang. There was nothing wrong at the time in investing large sums in Cuban sugar plantations or in having an American yacht club at Havana or in maintaining a naval base at Guantanamo after it had lost its usefulness as a guardian of the Panama Canal. But when nationalistic emotion reaches a certain temperature, the foreign presence causes irritation. Even a strong, developed, rational nation like Canada sometimes resents the fact that the huge influx of American capital, welcome and enriching, gives the United States too much weight in its affairs.

This, therefore, is not the era in which countries surrender sovereignty to an imperial power. Older nations pool sovereignties voluntarily for their own and the general good; weak ones may, willy-nilly, bow to superior military force. But the newly free zealously guard their independence against foreign domination. This answers the contention that if Russia released her East and Central European satellites they would become American satrapies or NATO bases directed against Russia. The ever-murky crystal ball of world politics reveals that a "people's democracy" unchained would disband collective farms, retain nationalized large industries, denationalize some small factories and almost all retail trade, and establish political democracy with, probably, a coalition of anticommunist social democrats and peasant parties opposed by a legal communist party. Its foreign policy would be strict neutrality except in the case of East Germany, whose wish for reunification with West Germany is frustrated only by the Soviet occupation. Yugoslavia, having escaped from the Soviet bloc, remained neutral, permitted capitalism in farming after village collectives were disbanded, and is conducting an interesting experiment in workers' management of factories—a kind of guild socialism.

The Soviet Union established its European empire between 1945 and 1949, when the United States enjoyed an atomic-bomb monopoly. What Stalin did in Eastern and Central Europe riled the West and contravened the Yalta and other agreements, yet he was not afraid. Moscow blockaded West Berlin by rail, road, and water (but not air) in 1948, before it had the A-bomb. It was not afraid of military retaliation by the United States. It cannot be afraid today. If the United States intended to attack the Soviet Union, the width of the satellite belt would offer no protection. Jets and rockets, by altering geography, also alter geopolitics. Colonies and satellites are no defense. Indeed, their discontents are a military and political liability. Nor is imperialism good economics. Electronics, atomic energy, automation, and antibiotics can contribute more than colonial profits to a country's prosperity.

Modern imperialism no longer makes sense except in terms of sentiment. The imperial power feeds its own national sentiment by frustrating that of the colony. Though this is the age of materialism, the emotions of masses play a decisive role in the decisions of statesmen. In some countries imperialism, because it builds patriotism, is still considered realistic domestic politics. It strengthens the government in office. It will for a while. After it the deluge.

Colonialism cannot win. "The era of imperialism is ended," U.S. Undersecretary of State Sumner Welles said at Arlington Cemetery on Memorial Day, 1942. The end began shortly after he spoke and has been coming nearer ever since. No power can block it. The end of imperialism will confer blessings on all mankind.

Imperialism, no matter how benevolent in intent or in fact, is a form of dictatorship and should have no place in a world that calls itself free. Relieved of colonies, the democracies will acquire a moral force to oppose the new imperialism of the dictators.

## chapter 8

# Nehru and the Future in India

JUST as sons and daughters yearn for independence though life under the parental roof may be sweet and advantageous, so territories claim freedom from colonialism without counting cost or loss. Recent history shows that this is not a matter to be argued rationally. Passions and a global tide wash away cold logic. A young generation of countries insists on setting up their own households.

This is the end and a beginning, and all beginnings are difficult.

The struggle for independence inevitably sired a revolution of expectations. The day Burma became free the capital city of Rangoon exhausted itself in festivities climaxed by a *Zst Pwe* play whose final scene showed people filling their pockets and pouches from a shower of gold and silver coins. Having depicted European domination as a system that stole the country's wealth and hampered its growth, what could be more human than to expect instant miracles after the foreigner's departure? The fulfillment of these hopes is a mandate to the leaders of the newly liberated countries.

Most colonial societies were stable, indeed stagnant. The penetration of imperial culture was gentle and superficial. Some individuals yielded to it and were transformed, but they did not bulk large in the great community. The sixteenth, perhaps even the fifteenth or tenth, century slept soundly while the twentieth century governed at the top and whispered politely to a limited class of native sons. Then came the ear-shattering tocsin of independence followed by the explosion of expectations. "We have suddenly arrived at a stage," Prime Minister Nehru said in 1950, "when we have to run. Walking is not enough, and in walking we stumble and fall and we try to get up again. It is no use anybody telling us to walk slowly. . . . It involves risks and dangers but there is no help and no choice for it, for there is torment in our minds." Given the tacit promise inherent in independence and the pervading, degrading poverty, Nehru's sense of urgency is easily understood. But "Make haste slowly." The Russians have a proverb, rarely heard nowadays in the Soviet Union, "The slower you go the further you get." Haste makes waste. The risks and dangers may exceed the possible gains. Nehru's "torment in our minds" is not the best equipment for careful planning. It is of course no use telling India to walk slowly; nobody does. The advice would be to walk fast instead of running and stumbling.

On March 3, 1960, Eugene R. Black, president of the International Bank for Reconstruction and Development (generally called the World Bank), speaking at Oxford University, chided underdeveloped countries that use economic aid for uneconomic purposes. He, who has allocated billions, complained of industries being established in Afro-Asia before markets existed to absorb their products and of irrigation systems in areas without a labor force to till the reclaimed land. One might add that sometimes beautiful college buildings stand idle for lack of teachers, students, and textbooks.

Urgency that leads, figuratively, to the building of a roof on stilts, without floors and foundation, is fatuous. Poor, weak countries are wasting their substance to satisfy dreams of glory and grandeur. Dictators and even democrats build themselves pyramids under the misty eyes of subjects drunk with unaccustomed patriotism. Industries, where it takes a tremendous outlay to create one workingman's job, are being fostered at the expense of the peasants, the bulk of the population, who cannot afford the investment. But rapid industrialization is the new Asian religion, and steel is god. A steel mill has come to be considered the indispensable badge of sovereignty. Without it a country cannot call itself free. Except in the case of India, imported steel would certainly cost less.

It is in this realm that former colonies might manifest their independence. Instead, they copy the West (which includes Russia) and race to catch up with nations beset by myriad problems because they are economically advanced. They forget that they fought for freedom to develop not only their material resources but also their national individuality.

Technology is indubitably necessary. It means food, health, shelter, and culture. Modernization spells survival. The retarded states must, willy-nilly, promote economic growth provided it begins literally on the ground, in the soil, in the village, which is the cellar of life, and can serve as the foundation of a new society. Hundreds of millions of Afro-Asian peasants live like animals, often with their animals in the same rude hut. They constitute the overwhelming majority of the population and deserve the nation's first concern. Farming methods can be improved and cottage industries expanded with little capital, thereby giving the peasantry fuller employment and diminishing the great exodus to already crowded cities where much idle labor breeds bigger and worse slums and tends to force the government into accelerated industrialization.

Nobody but a crank objects to industrial expansion. The point at issue is speed. The greater the speed the greater the exploitation, for foreign aid can never cover the entire cost

of the development. The people pay the major share in reduced consumption via inflation, higher prices, low wages,
and taxes. But hundreds of millions of Asians live so close
to austere subsistence that any lowering of standards would
entail acute suffering, disease, and political repercussions the
prospect of which might make governments tighten their
control over the population.

New governments usually prefer industrial construction
to less spectacular village development. Spending a hundred
million dollars on a steel mill is easier than helping a hundred
million peasants grow more rice. Conspicuous construction enthralls countries which feel poignantly that for centuries their light has been hidden under the bushel of colonialism. But what folly for a nation of villages to import
many million dollars' worth of food each year when better
seeds, plows, and bullocks, some rudimentary agricultural
information, and more tube wells would save those huge
sums for investment in factories and simultaneously produce
prosperous purchasers for the output of those factories.

Most socialists have always had a prejudice against what
Marx called "the idiocy" of village life. They regard the
peasant as a capitalist who must be reformed, organized,
propelled into collectives or co-operatives. Despite the demonstrably bleak economic results of collective farming in
Poland, the Soviet Union, Yugoslavia, and other communist
countries where it was a means of imposing political control
over the peasant the better to squeeze out of him the money
for urban industrialization, the government of India (and
Cuba) is strongly attracted to the herculean job of forming
village collectives or co-operatives. The probability is that
the peasants will not take to them. Faced with the choice of
using force or dropping the idea it will be dropped in India
as it was, sensibly, in Yugoslavia and, except on paper, in
Poland. Co-operatives are by definition, and by practice in

democratic countries, bodies voluntarily started and maintained by their own members. Governments are out of place
in this field.

Socialism has come to mean government participation in
economic affairs. The governments of numerous new states
build factories and dams with public money and hire officials
to manage them. The government, or the state, thus becomes the capitalist, and the system is state capitalism as
distinct from socialism under which, according to the original concept, society—that is, groups of citizens—would run
the economic enterprise where they worked and the state
would wither away. Under present-day "socialism" or state
capitalism the state does not wither away, it flowers. In these
circumstances bureaucracy expands. The result is bureaucratic imperialism. The proliferating bureaucracy seeks new
fields to conquer. An ever-increasing list of state-owned industrial installations is their standard of success and the
criterion by which they wish to be judged.

In one form or another—and the forms vary so widely that
they would not recognize one another—socialism was bound
to thrive in the former colonies. The colonies suffered from
imperialism. The imperialists were capitalists. Therefore an
anti-imperialist had to be an anticapitalist, in other words,
a socialist.

What the intellectuals of Asia could not blame on foreign
capitalists they blamed on their own domestic capitalists
whom they regarded as the worst of the breed. Many, not
all, native capitalists in backward countries were backward:
usurious moneylenders, or gouging shopkeepers, or predatory middlemen, or sweatshop manufacturers without the
social consciousness which their western counterparts had,
under the prod of legal enactments, trade unions, and enlightened self-interest, adopted as the twentieth century
grew older. Knowing capitalism in all its eighteenth- and

nineteenth-century ugliness, young nationalists who fought for independence usually made an automatic yet vague commitment to socialism and, often, to Karl Marx, whom few read; they saw him through the eyes of Laski or Lenin.

This attitude lingers on and helps to shape post-independence economic programs, domestic politics, and foreign policies. Thus the idea that a political party represents a social class dies hard even in Indonesia where, with as many as twenty-nine parties, nobody could find more than two or three or, maximum, four classes. Similarly, socialists affirmed that a communist country could not be imperialistic, and they called the first Leninist years of the Soviet revolution as their witness, only to be outraged by Russian annexations and subjugations during and after the Second World War and by Red China's incursions into Tibet and the violent seizure of Indian territory.

Gradually experience diluted the dogmas of the colonial period. Indigenous culture began to oust imported ideological weeds. The pluralistic Sukarno, in whose island country religion is a gaily colored palimpsest of animism, Hinduism, Buddhism, and Islam, calls himself a Marxist yet believes in horoscopes. His socialism is as different from Khrushchev's as Norman Thomas and Hugh Gaitskell are from Joseph Stalin. Bernard Kalb, reporting from Jakarta to the *New York Times* of March 2, 1960, conveyed the substance of an ideological discussion between President Sukarno and his guest, Prime Minister Nikita Khrushchev of the Soviet Union. Mr. Khrushchev had heard Sukarno speak so often of socialism that he finally asked for a definition. "Indonesian socialism," Sukarno explained, "is not severe socialism. It aims at a good life for all, with no exploitation."

"No, no, no," Khrushchev is said to have protested, "socialism should mean that every minute is calculated, a life built on calculation."

"That is the life of a robot," Sukarno commented.

Prime Minister U Nu of Burma became a socialist in the 1930's when it was the right thing to do. So did U Ba Swe, Burma's defense minister in 1952. In Rangoon I asked him at that time what he meant when he said he was a Marxist. "I find it difficult to explain," he replied. Finally, under further questioning, he declared, "I believe in it. In my student days it was the fashion, but I believe in it. It is a social philosophy and acts as guidance in the class war." When he first learned this lesson, Burma had no working class, middle class, or capitalist class, she was precapitalistic, and class war amounted to a nationalistic revolt against foreign capitalism, a struggle for independence. After independence, U Ba Swe saw this. "We cannot be a socialist state," he admitted to me, "without a proletariat, and to have a proletariat we must industrialize." U Nu went further. On January 29, 1958, he addressed the ruling party of his country for four and a half hours and dissected and rejected communism, Marxism, and state capitalism or socialism. Buddhism and the hard knocks of governing had banished youthful shibboleths. Now the Burmese government has formed partnerships with several British and Japanese private firms to exploit the resources of the country. If they existed, Burmese capitalists might do likewise.

University made Jayaprakash Narayan a Marxist. Handsome and tender—somewhat like Nehru in this respect—and with a stiff political spine, J.P., as Indians call him, led the Socialist Party of India in the 1940's and early 1950's until, after a three weeks' fast and the study of yoga, he declared himself a Gandhian. "For years," he said, "I worshiped at the shrine of the goddess of dialectical materialism. Now I have discovered goodness." He remains a socialist without Marxism, without materialism, without violence. Following Vinoba Bhave, Gandhi's spiritual heir, he has now dedicated his life to collecting land from the landed for the landless and, more recently, to founding voluntary village co-operatives in which peasants freely pool their farm strips, labor, implements, and animals for more efficient cultivation. Occasionally he steps out of this rural role into the arena of politics to chastise Nehru for a too tolerant attitude toward Soviet imperialism in Hungary and to condemn Chinese imperialism in Tibet. In India's favorite indoor sport, the guessing game called "After Nehru, who?" J.P. gets frequent mention. His prestige and influence grow, for he has renounced power in favor of service, and renunciation strikes a sympathetic chord in Indians. But having renounced power, J.P. does not wish to be prime minister after Nehru.

To govern is to change. To be Nehru is to change. The ideological pigeonhole where one might have found Nehru, off and on, in early manhood, does not hold him today. All his life he has indulged in stream-of-consciousness writing and speaking, in avowed groping, and in emotional and intellectual detachment. He rejected the domination of his remarkable, strong father, of the more remarkable, stronger Gandhi, his political father, and of the British. Yet his affection for all three was deep and abiding.

"Nehru is an Englishman," Gandhi once said to me. He is an Englishman and an Indian; an agnostic ruling over several hundred million religious Hindus and Moslems; an intellectual with little taste for power but a love for the drama, adulation, and stage-strutting that go with it; an indecisive man compelled to make decisions daily; a proud, impulsive, tempestuous person who nevertheless yields to argument and apologizes when he has caused pain; an apparently stubborn leader who bends to the demands of reality; a supreme egocentric yet an idealist.

Every facet of the highly polished gem that is Nehru

shines with several conflicting colors. "Here," he said of India on March 4, 1949, "we are committed to civil liberty in its broadest form. There can be no freedom in a country without a wide extension of civil liberties. We are also interning people without trial in large numbers and some of our provincial governments are passing legislation of a kind to which we took the greatest objection in the old [British] days." When friends complain about these practices they "find a certain echo in our minds."

A large part of Nehru is wedded to democracy. "My roots," he states, "are still perhaps in the nineteenth century, and I have been too much influenced by the humanist liberal tradition to get out of it completely." Reflecting Gandhism, but also many cognate philosophies, Nehru put to a UNESCO meeting in New Delhi on December 20, 1951, this rhetorical question: "Am I right in saying that the mental life of the world is in a process of deterioration, chiefly because the environment that has been created by the industrial revolution does not give time or opportunity to individuals to think?"

His goal, nevertheless, is a speedy industrial revolution for India, and part of Soviet Russia's early attraction for him lay in the rapidity of her industrialization which robbed individuals of the time and opportunity and indeed the right to think. Far back, in 1927, Nehru paid his first visit to the Soviet Union. He discovered that "the Soviet government has a special and ruthless way of treating its political opponents and all those whom it may suspect of counterrevolutionary activities." But he was cautious. "I shall not venture to pass judgment or to give final opinions," he wrote. "I too am impressionable and I must confess that the impressions I carried back with me from Moscow were very favorable and all my reading has confirmed these impressions, although there is much that I do not understand and much that I do not like or admire."

In the 1930's, in common with intellectuals in all continents, Nehru found fascination in Marxism. "Russia apart," he declared in *Toward Freedom,* his autobiography, "the theory and philosophy of Marxism lightened up many a dark corner of my mind. History came to have a new meaning for me. The Marxist interpretation threw a flood of light on it." A little later, however, in *Glimpses of World History,* he told Indira, his only child, that Marxism "is an attempt at reducing human history, past, present, and future, to a rigid logical system with something of the inevitability of fate or kismet about it."

"What is my philosophy of life?" he asked himself in the late 1930's. "I do not know. Some years earlier I would not have been so hesitant. . . . The events of the past few years in India, China, Europe, and all over the world have been confusing, upsetting, and distressing, and the future has become vague and shadowy and has lost that clearness of outline which it once possessed in my mind." The Second World War made matters worse. It brought him "many shocks, and adjustment was difficult. The Russo-German Pact, the Soviet's invasion of Finland, the friendly approach of Russia to Japan. Were there any principles, or any standards of conduct in the world, or was it all opportunism?"

Despite the shocks and doubts, Nehru still called himself a socialist. "The fundamental principles of socialism are acceptable to me," he asserted in 1948. The word "socialism" still wears a halo in Asia. On the other hand, Nehru knew, as he stated on March 4, 1949, that modern capitalism was "completely divorced from the old-style capitalism." The choice, therefore, was not between socialism and capitalism, for that would be a choice, he said, "between Soviet Russia and something which does not exist anywhere in the world. He was certain that "too much collectivism" destroys democracy, and "however much we may socialize our economy we do want to keep democracy."

Just as Soviet "Marxism," in Nehru's words on December 26, 1950, "has little to do with Marx," so Nehru's socialism is what he makes it. "I am not enamored of these isms," he said; and, on another occasion, "I do not care what ism it is that helps me . . . if one thing fails we will try another."

Speaking on November 28, 1959, at the inauguration, ironically enough, of a new section of the Harold Laski Institute of Political Science in Ahmedabad, Nehru said it was "rank nonsense" to apply Marxism to India. "The greatest revolution of today," he explained, "is atomic energy, a mighty force. Therefore a treatise of economic theories written before the industrial revolution would be out of date today." Some weeks earlier, on September 26, he had declared there was "less class difference in America today than in most countries of the world." India's aim too, he said, was a classless society.

Today, Nehru's and India's program is "socialist pattern." In introducing the key resolution at the 1955 convention of the ruling Congress Party, Maulana Abul Kalam Azad, Nehru's close friend and minister of education, said, "I would like to draw your attention, especially at this time, to the deliberate use of the phrase socialist pattern of society. This is most important because we want to have a socialist pattern and not socialism." What "socialist pattern" means and how it differs from socialism nobody has explained; both terms are equally elastic and opaque. Such imprecision has advantages, for a society feels uncomfortable in a doctrinal strait jacket and sooner or later manages to escape. The United States is no nearer to Adam Smith than Russia is to Marx and Engels. Then why should Nehru impale India on the piercing point of a dogma?

The outstanding feature of the socialist pattern is a government-made plan for the nation's economy. Planning has been Nehru's credo since pre-independence days. The plan drafted by the government, however, provides not only for what the state will do but also for what private enterprise will do. Nehru has no overflowing love of private businesses; he told a meeting of the Federation of Indian Chambers of Commerce and Industry in 1949 that "if your demands come in the way of the good of the masses, your demands will be completely ignored." He also charged that they were "not big enough to face the problems of the day." This may have been a reference to their stature and social consciousness, in which case it was an opinion. But Indian private enterprise certainly lacks the capital to erect giant hydroelectric power-irrigation projects. Therefore, the government builds them. Three big steel mills—one receiving funds and technical aid from the Soviet Union, a second from West Germany, a third from the United Kingdom—are governmental. The fourth, an extension of the iron and steel works in Jamshedpur owned by the billion-dollar private Tata corporation, was granted a large loan by the World Bank in Washington. This delineates the socialist pattern: state enterprise and private enterprise, as well as state partnerships with Indian and foreign firms. The balance of capital investment, however, is shifting in favor of the government. In 1961, according to a shrewd expert estimate, "two-thirds of the total capital invested in organized manufacturing will be private-owned and one-third government-owned." In the mid-1950's the government's share was only one-tenth.

A little "cold war" dialogue between state capitalism and

private capitalism fills the urban air of India. Businessmen complain that government encroachments discourage them from investing and expanding. Consequently, they contend, much capital remains "underground" and engages in fly-by-night transactions, quick moneylending, and speculation. Controls imposed by the burgeoning bureaucracy—there are already several million government employees in India—kill initiative and hamper development. The state not only controls private businesses; it competes with them and sometimes, so the argument continues, the very official who controls and investigates the private firm is the head of a government enterprise in the same business as the private firm. "He knows all our secrets and takes away our customers," an Indian capitalist complained. In launching the anti-State Capitalist, Welfare-Society Swatantra (Freedom) Party in 1960, Chakravarti Rajagopalachari, independent India's first governor general and a close friend of Gandhi's, stated: "I can tell you that the people today who are cultivators, merchants, traders, or industrialists are more afraid of the Congress Party government than they ever were of the British government with all its rifles. . . . They are afraid to speak out." There is a measure of justice in this. The government can give or withhold favors, orders, and credits.

But, the champions of state capitalism reply, India's shortage of foreign currency makes government supervision and licensing of imports and exports a national necessity. And since so much of industry depends on imports and exports, government controls tend to spread. Government planning for state and private enterprise likewise extends the area of government control. Moreover, the protagonists of the government-in-business submit, private enterprise is a petty, profit-mad, unenterprising vestige of the nineteenth century which leans too much on state credits and other forms of aid.

"I feel the charge that free enterprise in India has shown no initiative in recent years is hard to take," Mr. J. R. D. Tata, chairman of the Tata Iron and Steel Company, said in 1956. "I for one am in fact surprised at the amount of initiative displayed considering the discouragement and disincentives to which it has been subject." Similarly, Wilfred Malenbaum, head of the India Project of the Center for International Studies of the Massachusetts Institute of Technology, recently declared that "Indian industry in the last few years has demonstrated a vigor and vitality worthy of industry in the most developed lands. This vitality has been manifest in the private sector despite India's commitment to a socialistic pattern of society and a policy of increasing nationalization."

In the early years after independence, Nehru's attitude toward private business was part aristocratic snobbism, part theoretical predisposition. But even in the seventh decade of his life, when men's views tend to become sclerotic, he showed a remarkable evolutionary adaptability. What he wants above all is concrete results in raised living standards, not the testing of isms at the expense of emaciated people. "The whole philosophy behind this [Five Year] Plan," he told parliament in 1956, "is to take advantage of every possible way of growth." That includes private business. He rejected proposals which "satisfied some textbook maxim of a hundred years ago."

Nehru defined his economic views in a speech before the National Development Council in New Delhi on January 20, 1956. "Broadly speaking, of course," he said, "we all know our objectives and, so far as our Parliament and the Congress [party] organizations are concerned, they have laid them down very precisely as the socialistic pattern of society. Now, that is a broad indication, broad enough and yet precise enough about the direction in which we look. That is so, but even that can be interpreted in various ways. At any rate, the policies which may be laid down may be interpreted in various ways as to whether they are leading to that goal or not. Now, it becomes important that while on the one hand we do not wish to be doctrinaire about these matters—we have not, neither the Government nor the Congress [party], laid down any doctrinaire system of socialism, whatever they are—I need not go into them because all of you know—we do not want a rigid approach like people referring to some sacred text and saying 'we must do that because socialism means that.' That is not our approach. At the same time," he rambled on, "it is quite necessary that our approach should not be just a vague and muddleheaded use of the word 'socialism' without any content in that socialism. Nor is it to be just a mere expression of opinion. There has got to be some precise content about the goal, about the methods, and about the means and methods by which you seek to achieve that goal."

Coming closer to concreteness, he explained that "If you want India to industrialize and to go ahead, as we must, as it is essential, then you must industrialize and not bother about odd little factories producing hair oil and the like. . . . You must go to the root and the base and build up that root and base on which you will build up the structure of industrial India. Therefore, it is the heavy industries that count, nothing else. . . . We want planning for heavy machine-making industries and heavy industries; we want industries that will make heavy machines and we should set about them as rapidly as possible because it takes time."

In communist countries, "hair oil and the like" are planned. Every Soviet pin can be found in the plan. India's planning is not all-inclusive; it embraces heavy industry and Nehru added, the "control of essential minerals. . . . There has been much laxness in doling out leases of important min erals to private parties." He also wondered whether "important drugs should be controlled by the state."

Tata and Birla and other "private parties" are active in heavy industry and will probably continue so. Hair oil and the like, and textiles, and many other manufacturing branches remain the domain of individual capitalists and companies. Few private businesses in India have been nationalized. Private industry and government industry coexist and compete. The future of each depends on its efficiency and on political developments. India's Finance Minister Morarji Desai asks the West German government for transfusions of credits to help state enterprises. At the same time Mr. G. L. Mehta, former Indian ambassador in Washington, a critic of some Nehru ideas, goes to West Germany to obtain loans for his country's Industrial Credit Investment Corporation, which finances private enterprises. A wise division of the foreign aid given to India (and other underdeveloped lands) could tip the scales against totalitarianism.

Recently I discussed India and Austria with Dr. Bruno Pitterman, the Austrian vice-chancellor (deputy prime minister) who is the Socialist Party leader and the director of state enterprises. For many years Austria has been governed by a socialist-Catholic coalition which controls more than 90 per cent of the seats in parliament. The coalition is a carefully balanced construction: if a socialist is president of the state, a Catholic is chancellor and a socialist is vice-chancellor, and the various ministries are evenly divided because the two parties have almost equal electoral strength. In this Austria, which is more than 95 per cent Catholic yet almost 50 per cent socialist, over half of the industries, banks, power stations, etc., have long been nationalized. Nevertheless, Austria is a supremely democratic nation—and neutral though intellectually, sentimentally prowestern.

The great struggle in Austria is over the "Proporz"—the

proportion. A leading banker and former finance minister said that if the public sector of the economy rose above 50 per cent of the total it would be dangerous. He would like to reduce the Proporz somewhat. The socialists wish to maintain the present one-to-one relationship between public, or government, and private enterprise. Since the Catholic People's Party gets just under half the popular votes and since the socialists, who get about as many, are antitotalitarian, the Proporz is likely to remain such as to safeguard democracy and keep the economy a balanced public-private mixture. Under it Austria, a pauper rocked by ideological earthquakes after the First World War, has been rich and stable since the Second. Perhaps a mixed economy requires a political balance between socialists and nonsocialists.

India is a mixture of mixing and nonmixing. On the one hand, her long history of invaders (except the British) absorbed and of religions (except Christianity) ingested mirrors a capacity for unity in diversity, for merging, for tolerance. On the other hand, the caste system, Hinduism's starkest feature, represents isolation and breeds intolerance. The mixed economy now evolving in India, therefore, is less a sociological-cultural phenomenon than a requirement of all underdeveloped, capital-poor countries. These lands are short of everything but problems. If they nationalize private manufacture and trade they will curtail output, obstruct distribution, and multiply discontents. The guiding rule should be: Maximum production in the national interest, with safeguards for those who work. In Nehru's words: "Take advantage of every possible way of growth." To translate this into reality, Nehru in August, 1958, softened his government's attitude toward foreign investment. Through the wider opening in the floor, foreign investments have since doubled (with Britain first, West Germany second, and the United States third), thus bolstering Indian private capitalism.

In the late 1920's a great debate shook the Soviet Union. It concerned the future of the communist system. Bukharin, a recognized idealogue and member of the Politburo, publicly called on the mass of the population, the peasants, to "enrich yourselves." An opulent peasantry, he held, would enable the Soviet government to finance industrialization. Stalin sharply rebuffed Bukharin and later executed him. Stalin decided that a prosperous private-capitalistic farming class would strangle the communist dictatorship. Noncommunist countries in Asia, Africa, or Latin America do not face this problem. Therefore, their slogan can safely be "Full steam ahead for all branches of economy." Mixed economy plus balanced politics.

The motive of Soviet agrarian collectivization was not to give the country more food—it did just the opposite—but to chain the peasants to the state's farms and force them to sell a larger share of their crops to the government at low prices. The result of Stalin's simultaneous collectivization and industrialization program was his quarter century of terror. Alone the psychotic nature of Stalin would not explain the tightened tyranny of the 1930's, 1940's, and early 1950's. Soviet totalitarianism waxed as each five-year plan increased the speed of heavy industrialization, but not of consumer's goods production, and as village collectivization became total. Contrariwise, the 1956 bloodless Gomulka revolution in Poland, which brought an accession of freedom, coincided with a broad exodus from collective to private farms, a flowering of private trade, and a further deterioration of the morale in large government factories.

The interrelationship between liberty and economy is equally clear in democracies. Jayaprakash Narayan, the Gandhian ex-Marxist, has warned that rapid industrialization may have disastrous effects on representative government and civil rights in India. It has often been argued that people, especially hungry people in retarded countries, would prefer better living conditions to political freedom. This is not the alternative. The people in communist dictatorships were never asked their preference. They did indeed lose their political freedom; their governments grew strong; it is moot whether they achieved a better material situation at all commensurate with their effort and sacrifices. Under any other system, their rewards would have been far greater.

A lopsided economy distorted in the direction of heavy industries conduces to dictatorship. A lopsided economy based almost entirely on farming, and that too, as often in Latin America, on one crop—coffee, sugar, etc.—conduces to dictatorship. Democracy demands a political balance between the legislative, executive, and judicial branches of the government and an economic balance between agriculture, industry, and services. The difference between wealthy and poor nations may be judged by the number of persons engaged in these three economic divisions. The more affluent the country the fewer the persons on farms and the larger the number in industry and services: trade, transport, free professions, teaching, and so forth. Thus the agricultural population of Holland is only 12 per cent of the total, the industrial population 38 per cent, and the services population 50 per cent. In West Germany the corresponding figures are 12, 40, and 48; in Switzerland, 16, 46, and 38; in Austria, 22, 46, and 32. But, descending to poorer nations, the Italian figures are 40 for farming, 36 for industry, and only 24 for services; and Greece: 52, 22, and 26.

Of the 65,181,000 employed persons in the United States in July, 1958, 5 per cent were farmers and farm managers and 4.9 per cent farm laborers and foremen, according to the Bureau of the Census. The trend has been steeply downward. Roughly 10 per cent of America's gainfully employed produce far more food than America can consume. In the Soviet Union approximately half the population earns a living from agriculture. In India, more than 80 per cent.

It is equally true that the agricultural yield is greater where the agricultural population is smaller. Thus, the milk production in Holland is 4,000 liters per cow per year, in Italy 2,000 liters; in Holland the grain production per acre is twice Italy's.

High-yield farming helps finance industry, and both, when profitable, release more and more persons to serve the needs of comfort, leisure, and culture, and pursuits that approximate civilized living.

It might well be argued that life in the newly independent states of Asia and Africa and of the old nations of Latin America is difficult and cannot wait till balanced and prosperous economies are established by normal means. There are two answers: isms, whether capitalism, socialism, or communism, cannot hasten the process. Soviet history proves this. Toil and sweat and wise management, under maximum voluntary co-operation of the people, bring the best results. Secondly, the new economies enjoy the tremendous advantage of access to the science, experience, and aid of modernized foreign nations. Though they begin at the bottom, their climb could be facilitated by learning from the pioneers who did it the hard way. Some retarded countries that depend on bullock power are already reaching out to atomic power. The fruits of research, on which billions of dollars have been spent by technologically advanced countries, are Asia's and Africa's for the asking as soon as they can use them. Through the United Nations specialized agencies and other institutions, poor former colonies may avail themselves, gratis, of the world's best technical brains to help solve their problems. The key to a brighter future in India and elsewhere in Afro-

Asia is more skill in factories, more serious study in univers
ties, more attention to villages, less waste of manpower i
government offices, less interest in status and more in servic
less word patriotism and more work patriotism, less aggrai
dizement of state power and more improvement of individu
welfare.

---

## chapter 9

# *China, Pakistan, and India*

"WHAT does China want?" I asked.

"China wants to swallow us," replied the highly placed minister in Nehru's cabinet. He added something equally significant. "The menace of China," he said, "is generating more patriotism in India than the Kashmir issue or Pakistan ever did."

In Asia and Africa there is nationalism but there are no nations. The nations have yet to be born, and the newly independent governments see their task as the creation of that cohesion between all sections of the people which is the mark of nationhood. President Sukarno uses the Indonesian claim on Dutch-held New Guinea to foment anti-Dutch sentiment which will, he hopes, fertilize the seedbed of nationalism. Hostility to Israel serves a similar purpose for Arab leaders, and both India and Pakistan have sought to make nationalistic capital out of their dispute over the ownership of the Himalayan state of Kashmir. Not many inhabitants of southern India, however, care about northern Kashmir, and the poor anywhere in India are too immersed in their own daily tribulations to think of Kashmir. Besides, Pakistan is weaker than India. The meek Hindus, to be sure, have a traditional fear of Pakistan's martial Moslems. But modern warfare is less a matter of individual prowess than of technological progress, and in this India far outranks Pakistan. It is doubtful, therefore, whether Pakistan, the efforts of Nehru and Krishna

Menon notwithstanding, can arouse in Indians the fears an hates that are the diet of nationalism. Red China, on th other hand, has actually grabbed Indian territory and strong enough to grab more, and Nehru, after much hesita tion and long delay, branded her an aggressor. The Chin peril is enhanced by the support which Mao might obtai from Indian communists. The danger looks real and big. Th Indian nationalistic reaction is strong.

China remains an immediate as well as a long-range prob lem to India. The Nehru government has reinforced i military stations near the China border and is attempting t bolster the three tiny states of Nepal, Sikkim, and Bhutar which lie high in the mountains between India and Chin and may, because their people are more Tibetan-Mongolia than Indian, become the first targets of a further Chines military-political push southward into the Indian subcor tinent.

But far more drastic measures are needed to meet the cor tinuing challenge of China. The situation requires India an Pakistan to combine their armed forces for mutual defens against the Chinese.

An inspection of the map reveals that the Chinese conques of additional Indian territory could imperil the survival c Pakistan. Equally, a Chinese invasion of Pakistan would pu India in jeopardy. India and Pakistan are one by geography economy, and race, and the case, consequently, for joir defense in the face of China's bellicosity is unanswerabl Speaking in Kashmir, Vinoba Bhave, India's spiritual guid said, according to *Bhoodan* magazine of October 21, 195 "I am happy that General Ayub Khan [the president c Pakistan] has made an offer of common defense. But I woul like to add that common defense is not possible without common foreign policy. India is following a policy of noi alignment. Hence, if Pakistan continues to remain a membe of other alignments like the Baghdad Pact, how can there be a common defense?"

The point is well taken. Defense is nowadays so large a part of foreign policy that effective common defense requires a common foreign policy.

As a member of the Baghdad Pact (which, since the defection of Baghdad, has become CENTO) and of the Far-Eastern Alliance, or SEATO, Pakistan is aligned with the western powers against the communist alliance. India is nonaligned. This creates a foreign policy gulf obstructing the co-ordination of Indian and Pakistan defenses. From the point of view of peace and prosperity in Asia and of the struggle against red imperialism a common Indo-Pakistan defense is more desirable than Pakistan's membership in alliances which have little reality and more important than U.S. bases in Pakistan. It takes courage to give up what seems like a bird in the hand, but the reward would be considerable. It would alter the temper of the entire Afro-Asian world. A strong Asian front would be established against aggression in Asia.

America needs to re-evaluate her policy of alliances and bases. Time—the fellow traveler of technology—is the essential element in defense and foreign affairs. The United States, for instance, set up the Guantánamo naval base in Cuba in 1903 to protect the Panama Canal. That was in the age of the dinosaur, before the birth of bombers and when submarines had a maximum range of a few hundred miles. Today the Panama Canal could be defended from Connecticut and Michigan or not at all. Guantánamo should have been relinquished the moment Castro overthrew Batista's dictatorship. To have done so would have been a safe gamble, with possible salutary effects on Fidel's subsequent behavior. It is sometimes more blessed to give away. Seen in this perspective, and in view of India's alarm over Chinese aggression, the West and the world would gain by scrapping the policy of arming Pakistan, which most Indians mistakenly regard as an expression of American hostility toward them, and concentrating instead on reinforcing the inner defenses of both Pakistan and India.

American arms aid to some countries is a disguise for economic and budgetary assistance. The Congress in Washington eagerly opens its purse when asked for military assistance to foreign countries but is more reluctant to allocate funds for development. Having grasped this transparent truth, certain governments request and receive arms and finances for defense. Thus relieved of military expenditures they use the money saved for other purposes. India does just the opposite. She receives economic aid from the United States and uses the money saved for the purchase of armaments. In effect, therefore, the United States has been arming Pakistan against India and India against Pakistan. This is not an intelligent way to make appropriations, defend nations, fight communism, spread democracy, or fortify peace.

Vinoba Bhave, whose voice, after Nehru's, is the most influential in India, says, "Whereas Pakistan spends at least a hundred crores of rupees [approximately $200 million] every year on her army, India spends three times this amount on her army. Thus to spend four hundred crores of rupees on the army yearly is enormous." He added, "It is very painful to me that our right and left hands are both equipped with arms." To Bhave, the Pakistan and Indian armies are "our" right and left hands, the hands of one body. He made this specific. "I personally feel," he declared, "that India and Pakistan will have to come together, for the whole world is in the process of uniting. During the recent floods we witnessed that our rivers took logs worth crores of rupees to Pakistan. The rivers, the mountains, the floods are all giving us one message—'unite!' "

That Bhave was not speaking poetry but practical politics

is clear from his concrete proposal. "To me," he asserted, "the only solution of the Kashmir problem is the union of the two brother nations, India and Pakistan. Let them remain as two administrative units but let the three subjects: defense, foreign affairs, and communications, be common."

Pakistan has a strange configuration. Its western lobe, with approximately 38 million inhabitants, is one thousand miles from its eastern lobe, with 48 million inhabitants, and between them lies India with 420 million people. Mohammed Ali Jinnah, who fathered Pakistan, in 1947, vainly demanded a corridor between west and east Pakistan. Reunification in a confederation would open up a dozen, a hundred corridors.

India and Pakistan have been spending almost 50 per cent of their federal budgets on armaments, and their armed forces were, until the China invasion, emplaced to watch over one another. Each side declares that the other intends to make war on it because of the Kashmir dispute or for some other reason. These fears are either imaginary or, to the extent that they are real, ineradicable as long as the two countries remain twain.

Vinoba Bhave is not the only Indian leader who regrets the partition of his country. "It is a tragedy," Chakravarti Rajagopalachari, founder of the Swatantra Party, has said, "how what could have been such a great and prosperous and happy nation now stands divided and reduced to so painful a dependence after independence."

Nehru himself supports the idea of confederation. "Twenty years ago," he told Mr. Cyrus L. Sulzberger in an interview which the *New York Times* published on March 2, 1957, "I would have said that certainly we should have some kind of confederation, not federation—independent states with common defense and economic possibilities. . . . The difficulty now is if we talk about it. This upsets our neighbors [Pakistan] because we are so much bigger. Nevertheless, of course this remains the logical future path—confederation with each member maintaining its independence intact."

Confederation for common defense—with common communications and common foreign policy following automatically—would not be as difficult to achieve as might seem at first sight. "In actual life," Mahatma Gandhi said to me in 1942, "it is impossible to separate us into two nations. We are not two nations. Every Moslem will have a Hindu name if he goes back far enough in his family history. Every Moslem is merely a Hindu who has accepted Islam." Religion, to be sure, makes a difference, especially since Hindus and Moslems refrain from intermarrying and, often, because of varying dietary taboos, from interdining. But under British rule the Hindus, Sikhs, and Moslems in the Indian army ate at the same table and consumed the same kinds of food. They trained and fought in the same units and shared regimental loyalties. This was particularly true of the high-ranking officers who, whether Pakistanis or Indians now, are graduates of the Sandhurst Royal Military Academy or some other British training school, and have been steeped in the British military tradition of playing polo rather than politics.

In March, 1960, General Mohammad Musa, commander in chief of the Pakistan army, visited India, where he received from India's army chief of staff, General K. S. Thimayya, a painting depicting Sepoy Ali Haider, of the Frontier Force Regiment, storming a German position in World War II, an act for which the soldier won the Victoria Cross. On March 9, 1960, General Musa conveyed the painting to Ali Haider's battalion in Rawalpindi (Pakistan) and, with it, the best wishes from the officers of the same battalion now in India. The partition of British India into India and Pakistan tore the battalion in two, but its esprit de corps is intact, and it would not require much adjustment to reunite the halves. Certainly, the general staffs, consisting in some cases of old-

ime and wartime buddies, would happily pool their efforts
gainst China rather than unnaturally face one another in
ynthetic political hostility.

After the United Nations arranged a cease-fire to end the
ighting in Kashmir between the Indian and Pakistani armies,
he key figures of both met as old friends. "We met," General
Thimayya reported, "at the fifty-third milestone from Srinagar
o Muzzaffarabad. The Paks supplied dinner and beer. In
rder not to come emptyhanded, we brought delicious Kash-
nir apples. The first question asked me by the Pak officers
concerned the Indian girl who spoke on the local Indian radio
tation; they wanted to know if she was as lovely as her voice.
When I assured them that indeed she was, they sighed happily
and then got a basket of oranges for me to send to her." Comment on the folly of enmity would be wasted breath.

Mr. Rajeshwar Dayal, a member of the Indian Civil Service
under British rule, was the district magistrate of Mathura
during the Second World War when Captain Ayub Khan
served in the British army in the same area. The two men
were friends. Today, Rajeshwar Dayal, temporarily chief UN
administrator in the Congo, is Indian high commissioner
(ambassador) in Pakistan and Ayub Khan is president of
Pakistan. They speak the same language in many senses. Mr.
Brohi, Pakistan's high commissioner in New Delhi, is equally
at home among Indians.

Partition was superfluous surgery. Gandhi called it "vivisec-
tion" and opposed it to his death.

Before its birth, Mr. Mohammed Ali Jinnah called the
present Pakistan "quite impracticable" and "moth-eaten."
When Lord Louis Mountbatten, British viceroy at the time
of partition, showed Jinnah that to divide India the great
provinces of the Punjab and Bengal would have to be divided,
Jinnah, according to Mountbatten, was "horrified." Jinnah's
emotional reaction was correct; Bengal and the Punjab were

integrated entities. Yet they had to be bisected or there would
have been no Pakistan. So Jinnah acquiesced in the atrocity,
and both provinces as well as other areas ran with the blood
of hundreds of thousands. The wounds remain open and sup-
purate.

The undernourished, crowded hundreds of millions in
India and Pakistan pay every day in every way for the cutting
up of their subcontinent. Before independence in 1947, areas
now in Pakistan grew the jute which factories in what is now
India manufactured into the gunny sacks and burlap used for
packing throughout the world. After partition, India began
to grow jute and Pakistan built jute factories. Both countries
are too poor to afford such duplication. For raw materials
and machinery available cheaply in India, Pakistan goes to
remote continents. Pakistan depends on the waters of rivers
that rise in India. Partition separated vast farmlands from
their markets and cities from their rural hinterlands.

It would have been difficult, even in the best of circumstances, to lift undivided India out of her subnormal living
standard which, according to *Indiagram,* the bulletin of the
Indian embassy in Washington, allowed a "per capita income
at current prices" of $54.72 in 1955-56, $60.92 in 1957-58,
and $65.72 in 1958-59. If "at current prices" means at the
current prices of each year, then there may have been no
improvement at all. Moreover, these figures are averages for
the maharajah, the millionaire, and the farmer. A careful
study of a village which, having joined Vinoba Bhave's Gramdan movement, voluntarily pooled its land, labor, and animals,
reveals truly inhuman conditions. The village: Berain, in
the province of Bihar, with a population of 429, had an income before Gramdan of 45 rupees, or $9, a year per person.
After twelve months of co-operative agriculture, including
hand spinning and weaving to obviate the purchase of mill
textiles, the annual per capita income rose to 62 rupees, or

approximately $12.40. This advance from misery to slightly less misery warranted self-congratulation and national publicity. Bihar is a poor state and Berain a poor village. According to Indian government statistics, the average annual income per person in all villages was $36 in the first half of the 1950's and the same in the second half. Villages are 80 per cent of India and embrace rich landlords and landless paupers. In the same period the urban annual income average for everybody from the Nizam of Hyderabad and Mr. G. D. Birla to the Calcutta beggar rose from $160 to $200. For India plus Pakistan, in such poverty, to spend close to a billion dollars a year defending themselves against largely fictitious menaces attributed by each to the other is monumental folly if not criminal politics.

India and Pakistan are, though chiefly agrarian, short of food. India produced a record harvest of 73 million tons of cereals in 1959 and hopes to grow between 100 and 110 million tons in 1965. But that, according to a report by Ford Foundation experts, will be 28 million tons less than India will need in 1965 when her population shall have risen to 460 million. In part, said Indian Ambassador M. C. Chagla, speaking in Dallas, Texas, on May 16, 1960, this is due to increased consumption. But he added, "there is a more serious reason why our food production is lagging behind, and that is the constant and continuous increase of population. We grow more food and the population catches up with the increase." The ambassador, reading from the official text of his address distributed by his embassy, then alluded to the "massive aid" India had received from the United States, yet cautioned that "this economic aid will only bear fruit and produce full results if we can arrest the growth of our population." India, he stated, was "one of the few countries in the world which has officially at governmental level adopted the policy of birth control and family planning. We have earmarked a sum of about $200 million in our Third Five-Year Plan. What we want to achieve is to cut down our birth rate"—which is not high by American or western standards—"by at least half."

To attain this goal, Ambassador Chagla asserted, "I think that what we really need in India today is a cheap oral contraceptive." Here he asked for assistance from the United States government. "I know," he declared, "that private agencies in this country"—the United States—"have been working at producing such a pill, but unless the government here officially steps in the help that we would expect from this country would indeed be infinitesimal. If the government"—of the United States—"gives the green light, then India can benefit by all the scientific knowledge that this country has and help us to produce either the cheap oral contraceptive I have been speaking about or something equally cheap and effective."

Chagla, a great jurist, was fully aware of the explosive effect his remarks might have on American domestic politics. Yet he affirmed unequivocally, "This country says that she wants to remain neutral on the question of birth control and family planning in India. I say to you with all the emphasis I can command that on a question like this a great country like the United States cannot afford to be neutral."

When a highly responsible, supremely intelligent diplomat speaks in such stern terms it is easy to imagine how desperate India's economic situation is and will remain despite the very numerous visible achievements. Pakistan has the same problem and takes the same view of it. "Planning for a sensible size of family is a vital condition of progress to prosperity," Ayub Khan said on December 30, 1959. Pakistan's 2 per cent growth in population per year, he declared, was "a matter of grave urgency."

The addition of Pakistan to India, it might be argued,

would only multiply the headaches. This is a superficial view. India and Pakistan as separate nations separately administered would, after confederation, still confront myriad towering problems. But the waste of two defense systems, of two conflicting foreign policies, of two economies competing in futile enmity, of two water systems, and of railways that lead nowhere will have been eliminated. The Kashmir issue, which has bedeviled Indo-Pakistan relations for more than a decade, also would vanish. Kashmir could, by self-determination, be a third member of the confederation, indeed the confederation capital—a sort of Washington, D.C. This is very different from the independence for Kashmir proposed in the past by some circles. An autonomous Kashmir might have become a bone of contention between feuding India and Pakistan. But with the two countries joined for mutual benefit, Kashmir would serve them as a bridge rather than a battlefield. An independent Kashmir, moreover, might have tempted Russia or China to intrigue and infiltrate and fish for influence and footholds from which to menace both India and Pakistan. Kashmir in a confederation will inhibit the northern imperialists.

Confederation would correct the 1947 blunder of allowing religious politics to sever India from Pakistan. Many officials and citizens of both countries have discovered that the expected benefits of bisection were illusory. Their disappointment reveals more clearly than elsewhere the chasm between the grim reality of national independence and the dreams of golden glory which preceded it. Today, however, nobody would, and nobody can, turn back the clock to colonial dependence. It can only be advanced to some form of interdependence between the two neighbor-brothers.

The history of India's partition in 1947 is now well documented. The British Labour government opposed partition. A British cabinet mission, consisting of Sir Stafford Cripps,

Lord Pethick-Lawrence, secretary of state for India, and Mr. A. V. Alexander, first lord of the admiralty, arrived in New Delhi on March 24, 1946, and, after consulting all parties and many representative individuals, published its plan on May 16 with explanatory comments. The mission stated that it had examined "closely and impartially the possibility of a partition of India" but found that division of the country would weaken its defense and tear its transport system in two. "We," the three ministers wrote, "are therefore unable to advise the British government that the power which at present resides in British hands should be handed over to two entirely separate sovereign states." Instead, the high-ranking British Labourites recommended a confederated India with one government to manage foreign affairs, defense, and communications, and leaving all other subjects to the members of the confederation. Maulana Abul Kalam Azad, the president of the Congress Party at the time of the negotiations with the British cabinet mission, and subsequently minister of education in independent India, published an autobiographical book, *India Wins Freedom,* in 1958, which, though dedicated to Nehru to whom Azad was devoted, blames Nehru as well as Vallabhbhai Patel, the "strong man" of the Congress Party, for acquiescing unnecessarily in partition after giving Jinnah, the Moslem League leader, the opportunity to insist on it. When Azad's book appeared, Nehru, with customary magnanimity, did not deny the validity of the accusation. In 1949, in fact, Nehru had said publicly in New York he would have resisted partition had he anticipated the dire results that flowed from it.

Prime Minister Jawaharlal Nehru frequently chides western statesmen for lacking the imagination, good will, and courage to overcome the obstacles to friendly relations between their countries and the communist bloc. He was seventy years old on November 17, 1959, and, though amazingly virile in India's debilitating natural and political climate, he cannot hold the reins of power many more years. He might himself, therefore, particularly in view of what he has called China's "deliberate program of aggression," indulge in an exercise of imagination, good will, and courage and act now to forge new bonds with Pakistan. This can best be brought about by a leader as popular as Nehru.

Nehru is, in fact, king. We live in a monarchical era. Nehru is king. Tito is king. De Gaulle is king. Adenauer is king. Macmillan would be king if there were no queen. Nehru reigns and rules and can remain in office as long as he has the wish and the necessary physical and mental capacity. His power is so great that, but for his addiction to democracy, he would be a dictator; no opposition can make an effective stand against him. He undermined the Socialist Party opposition by adopting the "socialist pattern" and moderates communist antagonism by praising the Soviet Union. A lesser Indian leader would perhaps allow the forces of democracy in parliament, the public, and the press freer play; it is unwise to guess. The assumption that India thanks her democracy to Nehru alone is equally unwise. In any case, Nehru could, if he cared, confederate with Pakistan, and he might find the opposition and obstacles surprisingly small.

On the Pakistani side, President Ayub Khan likewise has the power to settle the conflict with India. A Pakistani foreign minister once told me that he and his prime minister would be assassinated were they to come to an agreement with India which did not give them satisfaction on Kashmir. No one knows the future. But Ayub, the dictator, can dare to do what his undemocratic predecessors failed to do.

The idea that a general who disbands parliament and dismisses the government has thereby abolished democracy is facile and fallacious. Pakistan had never been a democracy before Ayub seized power in October, 1958. Pakistan had never had a national election for parliament or president or anything else. The statement in a propaganda leaflet of the Ayub era that, "A band of unscrupulous politicians, for the sake of personal gain and glory, had landed the nation into a labyrinth" is true if "labyrinth" may be translated "political and economic mess," and if "glory" is deleted. For the band came to an inglorious end. Ayub faced all previous ministers with the alternative of avowing their malfeasance or inviting investigation and, if warranted, prosecution. Thereupon the prime minister whom Ayub supplanted disclosed where he personally was hoarding 3,000 tons of grain for speculation. He was not the worst sinner in the farflung official family.

Corruption in high and low political places is an ugly feature of many governments, democratic and totalitarian, Occidental and Oriental. How much more so in underdeveloped countries where, because of limited employment opportunities, a turn of the political screw may eject a minister or lesser luminary from a well-paid post into lifelong idleness? He therefore harvests while the sun shines, knowing that with wealth, however ill-gotten, goes the social status all men, especially Asians, crave. Top Indian officials, bred on Gandhian ethics, and others in the East in whom idealism or power sublimates greed, are the exceptions. The military too, wedded to the tradition of national service and inured to modest emoluments, may spurn corruption during the first flush of their crusade to stamp it out. Military dictatorships do seem to have a justifiable function as cleansers and caretakers. General Ne Win, when he imposed army rule in Burma in 1958 at the request of Prime Minister U Nu, purged the state apparatus of many idlers, blunderers, and financial gangsters, and did something more which only a temporary regime immune to popular outcries could attempt: he removed from the streets of the capital tens of thousands of refugee-squatters who threatened to make Rangoon a rival

for Calcutta's crown as the filthiest city on earth. Then the
army supervised the elections which returned U Nu to his
high office. The 1960 Turkish revolt staged by intellectuals—
university professors and students and middle-class, educated
army officers—likewise promised to hold power until elections.
Iran, rich in oil revenues that rarely trickle down from the
thin, blind, brittle, feudal upper crust to the indigent tribes-
men and peasants, is another country ripe for revolution
against undemocracy. The Shah, though the pinnacle and
symbol of the present corrupt structure, could afford to introduce at least a semblance of freedom by sweeping out the
political filth. His western allies would be doing him a service
if they whispered this into his ear.

Ayub Khan in Pakistan has undertaken a more protracted
task with a deeper purpose. He proposes to create the basis,
where none exists, of a true, viable democracy. Independent
India began life equipped with the Gandhian philosophy of
the individual-above-all and committed to secular rule, social
reform, and economic planning which Nehru and many other
leading Indians had long advocated. But Pakistan came into
this world naked except for one word: Islam. This might have
sufficed. Yet, as President Ayub Khan has himself written,
"In our ignorance we began to regard the Islamic ideology
as synonymous with bigotry and theocracy, and subconsciously
began to fight shy of it." Islamic ideology seemed an anti-
quated guide for a twentieth-century state, and Pakistan,
having no substitute, rocked like a rudderless raft in a hurri-
cane. Pre-Ayub, Pakistan's character was shaped by backward
mullahs (Moslem teachers) and rich landlords.

The landlord in feudal Asia does not merely own a big
estate, he owns the souls of the peasants who cultivate it and
he can intimidate them and influence their political actions.
While it is true that in India and elsewhere voters may sell
their votes to the highest bidder and then go into the secret

ballot booth and vote for his opponent, the delivery of an entire village's ballots to the favored candidate of the major local landlord is far from an isolated phenomenon. Land reform, plus of course education and freedom from mullah domination, but above all land reform, is thus the indispensable preliminary to Pakistan free elections. In Pakistan, as in most of Asia, except in uncrowded Burma and Siam, a land reform is the *sine qua non* of material progress and democracy. Where, however, as in Pakistan (and today in the Philippines) all the political parties in parliament were controlled by landlords who stand to suffer from a land reform, no such reform could be legislated. No sooner had Ayub Khan come to power and dissolved parliament than he instituted village changes. "The power of the big landlords in West Pakistan, who have prevented all real reform for the past years, is broken," Kingsley Martin wrote from Pakistan —the London *New Statesman and Nation,* April 10, 1960. "A ceiling has been placed on land-holdings and the big estates—often amounting to tens of thousands of acres—are being divided amongst the cultivators." After a long talk with Ayub Khan, editor Martin, who is only slightly less allergic to dictators than I, credited the general with "massive common sense" and "subtlety." "I know of no other dictatorship," Martin declared, "that has been set up without bloodshed and with so little bitterness. No one has been killed and I'm told that there are now no political prisoners in Pakistan." When Nehru heard of Ayub's land reform, he commented, "I am personally very happy about it as it would benefit a vast number of people in Pakistan."

India's first reaction to Ayub Khan's seizure of power was primitive alarm. Second thoughts and further observation improved relations between the two countries. There have been agreements about finances. As Ayub's social profile emerges, he wins praise and makes friends in India. Most remarkable is President Ayub Khan's arrival, after a career several million light miles removed from that of Gandhi, at a basic tenet of the Mahatma's philosophy. Vinoba Bhave and Jayaprakash Narayan have been advocating its adoption by India. Ayub Khan, in whom the idea probably matured without outside prompting, is actually putting it into practice. This innovation, applicable to Asia and Africa, and perhaps to Latin America, spells nothing less than a political revolution; it assumes that political parties are obsolete, antidemocratic, and ripe for burial.

A member of Nehru's cabinet, touring the state of Bihar recently, heard from peasants that India was ruled by a king named Nehru who would be succeeded, when he died, by his son. (Nehru has no son.) Another high Indian government official on a visit to northern India found peasants not yet aware of the departure of the British raj. Illiteracy and ignorance are not the only circumstances which militate against democratic effectiveness. Parties in Asian and African countries and even in western nations may be manipulated by self-seeking, sometimes self-perpetuating oligarchies which make a mockery of popular government. But the chief contention of Vinoba Bhave, Jayaprakash Narayan, and other Gandhians is that party alignments split the village unnaturally into feuding segments which have no relation to its acute, intimate problems. Why divide the village electorate along party lines during the choice of a member of parliament, who will go to remote New Delhi to support or not support Nehru's economic plan or foreign policy, and then transfer these divisions into village elections where the important, in fact almost only, consideration should be whether the members of the village panchayat, or council, possess qualities of leadership, arouse trust, and can solve day-to-day down-to-earth problems? Vinoba and Jayaprakash therefore propose party-less village council elections. The village councils of a district will then elect a district council. The district councils of a county will elect a county council. A group of county councils will elect a state council, and state councils will elect a federal council or parliament—the central government. When Gandhi sketched this electoral pyramid to me in 1942, I told him this was the soviet system (the Russian word "soviet" means council), to which he replied, "I didn't know that." The Russian soviets were actually very democratic institutions until, soon after seizing power in November, 1917, the bolsheviks used compulsion to make them tools of totalitarianism. Such a danger would have to be avoided if the scheme were applied in India. "Common sense dictator" General Ayub Khan has introduced the council plan in Pakistan. If it works it will decentralize political power, curb the functions and prerogatives of the federal and state bureaucratic imperialists, diminish state capitalism, and, with more local responsibility, accelerate education in democratic government. I can think of no Asian government that would not benefit from this innovation. Gandhi advocated it for India as a guarantee against dictatorship. The very un-Gandhian dictator of Pakistan is, strangely enough, translating it into life. Could this create another channel of sympathy between India and Pakistan?

Ayub Khan has also tried to close the gap separating his country from Nehru's by pressing for a solution of the painful Kashmir problem. While Kashmir remains torn in two, with the Indian army holding the larger part and the Pakistani army the smaller, friendship is impossible and common defense unthinkable. Ayub says, "I have met Mr. Nehru and some other sensible leaders. We are doing our best to explain our point of view to these leaders and persuade them to see the necessity of settling this question. For it appears to me as a student of history that if this question is not solved it may end in the ruination of Pakistan and India and both may even lose their independence." Plainly, he was alluding to the menace of China, which will grow as long as the two segments of the Indian subcontinent face inward in mutual hostility instead of outward in self-defense.

The World Bank, one of the least-known and most-effective agents of twentieth-century internationalism, has made a mammoth contribution to the settlement of the Kashmir issue and thus to Indo-Pakistan co-operation. Five of the great rivers of the Indus River basin—the Jhelum, Ravi, Sutlej, Chenab, and Beas—rise in India-held Kashmir and are indispensable to the life of Pakistan and India. In April, 1948, India, because of the Kashmir mess, cut off the waters from these rivers that feed the canals of Pakistan. Long negotiations between the two disputants yielded no fruit. Then the World Bank quietly appeared on the scene and proposed the construction of a tremendously intricate and fabulously expensive system of dams, storage reservoirs, and canals which, without diminishing India's water supply, would satisfy the needs of Pakistan. Years of patient poring over blueprints, budgets, and memoranda followed until, in 1960, mutual accommodation was achieved. The new water network, to be completed in ten years, will cost more than a billion dollars. The United States, Great Britain, West Germany, Canada, Australia, and New Zealand, plus India and Pakistan, have undertaken to furnish this sum, and the World Bank will manage it. Much of the expense and heartache would have been avoided had there been no partition. But this is stale water over old dams. The important thing is that the rivers and canals say, "Unite." Common sense says, "Unite." China's policy says, "Unite." Survival says, "Unite."

"The reason why communist China is committing aggression against India is that it wants to secure 'positions' on India's natural frontiers in order to make India completely vulnerable. . . . China has a feeling that if India, Asia's only remaining bastion of democracy, could be humbled and humiliated, it would be easy for her to subjugate the rest of the continent. . . . The threat from China, therefore, is no momentary aberration. It is planned strategy to impose communist ideology on unwilling people." These are the words of Asoka Mehta, brilliant thinker, member of the Indian parliament, leader of the Socialist Party, and a partisan of Nehru's foreign policy of nonalignment.

China's advance to the mountain passes that open into the Indian plains may, therefore, enlighten the Indian government and people on the rude reality of world affairs. After China's penetration into Tibet and India, Nehru wrote in an article published by the *New York Times* on March 11, 1956, "Geography made India, in her long past, almost a closed country. Surrounded by the sea and the mighty Himalayas, it was not easy of entry." This is bad history. India has been invaded more than twenty times since antiquity. Yet Nehru's foreign policy was molded, to a considerable extent, by the illusion of inaccessibility. Many Indians have a tendency to escape into the comfort of illusion. Faced with the concrete fact of China's seizure of Indian territory, they can no longer do so. Nehru has drawn some of the consequences of the awakening. Reacting to events and to angry public opinion at home, he has expressed not only disapproval of China's acts but distrust of Chinese words. Chinese Prime Minister Chou En-lai "told me," Nehru reported in parliament on April 27, 1959, "that while Tibet has long been a part of the Chinese state, they did not consider Tibet as a province of China." Nehru would not lie about his talks with Chou, who was obviously seeking to mislead. Tibet is today a province under Chou's heel.

The Indian Prime Minister may now accord western foreign policy a little more understanding. "The tensions and conflicts which we see in the world today," said an Indian spokesman of Nehru, addressing an American audience in May, 1960, "are due to the fact that we [meaning you] are not prepared to tolerate and live with people different from ourselves and systems of government which we do not approve." This, to put it plainly, is untrue, and it is about time, after their experience with China, that Indians see the light. Western antagonism to Russia is due not to ideology but to Soviet imperialist expansion. During and immediately after the Second World War, the western powers made the same mistakes that India made in relations with China after 1954: they hesitated to assess correctly the ugly facts of life; they appeased; they rearmed reluctantly and haltingly. The Indian government showed more than tolerance of China's different system of government (as America did of Russia's) and more than tolerance of China's aggression (as the West did of Moscow's). But Mao and Chou were not deterred. Perhaps they were even encouraged by Nehru's softness and nonalignment.

To retain its posture of nationalism the Indian leadership will be forced, despite strong inhibitions, to compose the differences with Pakistan and oppose Chinese penetration.

In this terrible dilemma for India—and all Indians would rather feed and build than arm—the Indian government must hope that Russia can restrain China. At the height of India's —and Indonesia's—trouble with Mao, Khrushchev urged the inclusion of both those countries in summit and other high-level deliberations. Such gestures were naturally interpreted in New Delhi as reflecting a divergence between Russia and China which justified India's continued aloofness from a western alignment. It may indeed have been the purpose of Khrushchev to create that impression. The Indian government presumably knows that the United States, through the United Nations, would defend India in case of a Chinese attack. But it must logically be New Delhi's hope that Moscow could prevent the attack. In these circumstances the West would do well to help and wait but not to push. India embraces approximately half, and with Pakistan more than half, the population of the underdeveloped Afro-Asian world. This makes India a central and perhaps the most delicate problem of our aching world. She should not be hurried.

## chapter 10

# *A Matter of Love*

THE primary problem of all newly independent countries, and of most old countries, is administration. Economics are supremely important. But without efficient administration there is no successful economy. It was the breakdown of administration, of government authority, of law and order, not of the economy, that enabled the bolsheviks in Russia and Mao in China to seize power. Likewise, the establishment of communist rule in the Indian state of Kerala—the only instance in history when communists took office by democratic means—was due to the temporary absence of an alternative political combination that could govern. France, on the other hand, proves that economic prosperity is no guarantee of stability. With all her economic well-being, France needed de Gaulle's authority to keep the administration stable.

The new African states face a most complicated administrative task, first, because they are tribal, and therefore fragmented, societies and, second, because they lack trained administrators. When the British left India there remained behind an effective Indian civil service, police, and non-political army which they had trained. The Dutch bequeathed no such treasure to Indonesia. This is one explanation of subsequent Indian order and Indonesian confusion. On achieving independence on June 30, 1960, the Congo had seventeen university graduates, not one native physician, a sergeant major as her highest-ranking soldier, and few government employees above the level of messenger and clerk. Small wonder that the Congo was born in bloodshed.

Bad administrators dislike criticism, dislike parliament, love secrecy and compulsion. They tend toward dictatorship. Actual disturbances or anticipated difficulties conduce to dictatorships. Most leaders of African independence movements expect to become, and become, dictators. Said Julius Nyeyere, who, the *New York Times* predicted, would be the prime minister of independent Tanganyika, "No one should be surprised to see that the first governments [of new African states] will be largely one-party governments." And one man usually dominates the one party. The Congo achieved the other extreme and therefore extreme maladministration: in her 1960 elections more than ninety parties, each representing a tribe, put forward their candidates for parliament.

The central fact about Africa south of the Sahara is tribes. "African social structure," wrote Tom Mboya, Kenya's outstanding Negro, in the April 25, 1960, *New Leader,* "is based in the main on the tribal unit within which is the clan, and below this the family. Some tribes own land on a tribal basis, others on a clan basis, and only very few have a family identity. Socially, members of a tribe regard each other as brothers and sisters, whatever their actual relationship may be. They own and use their land and other property, such as cattle, communally."

To win independence, the one man has only to incite the tribes against the white ruler. To enjoy independence, he must curb them if he can. Then begins the long, breathless climb to nationhood.

African tribal organization wraps together blood ties, economic survival, and the gods. The enemy, if any, is the neighboring tribe, not the next-door country or unknown America or Russia, much less communism, socialism and capitalism, which are beyond comprehension. To the extent that the

African was aware of foreign rule it meant a white man whose gun obstructed natural tribal rivalry. The independent government that replaces the colonial administration must substitute a new mailed fist and add a silver tongue. No sooner do the tribes note the departure of the foreign master than they begin to compete with, sometimes to fight, one another. The president or prime minister of the new African state is a member of one tribe. But he will rule over all tribes. This starts feuds. To be subjects of a remote white king or queen or president is one thing. To submit to the chief of a rival tribe is galling.

Ghana won independence on March 6, 1957, and chose to remain in the Commonwealth. Now Ghana had a big national chief—Kwame Nkrumah—who was bigger than the tribal chiefs. He insisted, of necessity, on their allegiance and obedience. Everywhere in Africa the intellectual and political elite—the new ruling class—clashes with the hereditary tribal elite. The program of the nationalists is detribalization, for tribal loyalties limit national unity and tribal customs hamper economic and social evolution. Inevitably, friction arises between the traditional order and the new order. The tribes sense intuitively that nationalism threatens, and may ultimately supplant, their way of life. In Ghana, accordingly, the parliamentary opposition proposed an "elective monarchy" headed, in rotation, by one of the country's six paramount tribal chiefs. Nkrumah's majority recognized this as a move against him, as a tribal gambit against the central authority, and voted it down. In the Congo, similarly, a United States of the Congo—a federation of provinces generally coterminous with tribal domains—was a widespread wish which, when frustrated, stoked the fires of Katanga separatism and secessionist movements in the lands of the Baluba, the Lulua, and other tribes. But Prime Minister Lumumba preferred a strong central government and a unitary, rather than a federal, system on the ground that they were the only way to prevent tribal warfare, promote efficient administration, and preserve his personal power. Federation would be the sensible solution in the Congo—as in Indonesia. But federalism awakens false, unfortunate fears of imperialist intrigues to keep a foothold in the former colony.

Black Africa, a congeries of myriad tribes, is plagued with more than a thousand languages, as well as a thousand dialects, and the languages are so different, though spoken by neighboring peoples, that the master of one usually cannot speak another. A tribe may occupy a compact territory or be dispersed over a wide area. A tribal map of Nigeria (population 39 million; annual income per person $84) shows segments of the same tribe living in geographical pockets hundreds of miles apart. Some African tribes are sedentary, some nomadic, and the nomads may be farmers as well as herdsmen. Africa is not a cattle continent; the tsetse fly has halved herds and flocks in numerous districts. The soil in most parts of Africa is so poor that a single crop may exhaust its fertility; the only fertilizer available is the ash left from the burning of the jungle. Since land, though inferior in quality, is plentiful and population density low, clans and families often move from one farming area to another and back again. This militates against easy administration. African nomads, like Arab Bedouins, neither understand nor respect national frontiers. The British have always allowed members of the great Masai tribe to wander at will between British Kenya and British Tanganyika. The prospect of independence for both these colonies is already alarming the Masai and they have asked London whether their nomadic rights will be guaranteed when Kenya and Tanganyika are ruled by different, national governments. Sir Patrick Renison, British governor of Kenya, told a gathering of Masai chiefs on July 11, 1960, that they would have to "modify their way of life" and "think in terms of playing their full part in the politics and economics of Kenya rather than in terms of seeking to separate from Kenya." Wise but unheeded words, for at a subsequent jamboree the chiefs resolved that the Masai wanted to live in one independent state, not in two. Elsewhere, tribes sitting astride the boundaries of two countries tend to take the same view. Part of the Sanwi tribes lives in Ghana, part in the Ivory Coast. Some Sanwi are in Accra, Nkrumah's capital, demanding union with Ghana. The government of the Ivory Coast is suspicious. Part of Togoland voted in 1956 to join Ghana. Now newly independent Togoland, a former French colony, wants its own back, and the question has been debated whether Ghana will annex the rump of Togoland or release its Togoland section to join the rump. Meanwhile, Premier Sylvanus Olympio of Togoland calls Nkrumah "a black imperialist."

Tribalism breeds economic problems too. In the African social structure, writes Tom Mboya, "greater production is not necessarily the main or immediate objective. African wealth takes the form of cattle, goats, and sheep, not necessarily for sale and slaughter, but for such purposes as dowry payments and ceremonial fees." Where wealth is for show and not for sale, where landownership is tribal, there can be no capital and hence no private capitalism or state capitalism. In northern Ghana all land belongs to the earth-god, the object of religious worship. Priests administer the land for the god and dole it out to the tiller.

When Ghana was the Gold Coast, the British did not permit foreigners to acquire land. The tribes held most of the land—except in the north—and individual farmers cultivated a small patch to produce either cocoa or food. Cocoa, the big export crop, requires little labor. The Ghanaian watches the beans grow and picks the ripe ones. When it was argued that large cocoa plantations would operate more efficiently, Sir

Hugh Clifford, a former British governor, replied, "A plantation system is not a society; it is an economic agglomeration created for the pursuit of profit. It substitutes itself for those primitive societies which in sickness and health sustain their members."

One can imagine a tribal chief, if he had the sophistication and education, making a similar reply to post-independence social modernizers who would scrap tribal economics. The roots of the old go very deep. In the shade of the tribal tree the African finds security, social warmth, and a satisfying communal culture. Yet the protagonists of progress, knowing from personal experience the virtues of tribal life, know too that it prevents national cohesion and economic growth. They are pressing for quick change.

Young men, usually without women, go to slum towns to seek work. They are only partially detribalized, for they retain strong ties with their tribes, whence they ultimately get wives and to which they often return after middle age. The only fully detribalized elements in Black Africa are government officials, the few professional persons and intellectuals, many of them trained abroad, as well as merchants. These, constituting perhaps 1 or 2 per cent of the national population, are the nationalists, the national bourgeoisie, and the majority of them pay lip service to socialism.

In 1960, when Nehru was seventy, Tom Mboya of Kenya was twenty-nine, Patrice Emergy Lumumba of the Congo was thirty-four, Julius Nyeyere of Tanganyika was thirty-eight, President Sekou Touré of Guinea was thirty-eight, Sir Abubakar Tafawa Balewa of Nigeria, Africa's largest state, was forty-seven, and Prime Minister Nkrumah of Ghana was fifty-one. Because of age or lack of opportunity, they missed the "Marxist Thirties" in Europe. Nevertheless, some of them adopted Marxism even in the 1940's and 1950's when its vogue in the West had passed.

Nkrumah, for instance, said, "I am a nondenominational Christian and a Marxist socialist and I have not found any contradiction between them." In the United States he attended universities, worked as a bellboy, welder, sailor, and dishwasher, and studied the methods of Democrats, Republicans, communists, and Trotskyists. "I read Hegel, Karl Marx, Engels, Lenin, and Mazzini," he wrote in his 1957 autobiography. "The writings of these men did much to influence me in my revolutionary ideas and activities, and Karl Marx and Lenin particularly impressed me." Later, in London, "I devoted much energy to the study of revolutionaries and their methods. Those who interested me most were Hannibal, Cromwell, Napoleon, Lenin, Mazzini, Mussolini, and Hitler. . . . At first I could not understand how Gandhi's philosophy of nonviolence could possibly be effective. . . . The solution of the colonial problem, as I saw it at that time, lay in armed rebellion. After months of studying Gandhi's policy and watching the effect it had, I began to see that, when backed by a strong political organization, it could be the solution of the colonial problem."

The Ghana leader, nothing but frank, was obviously shopping around for a method rather than a philosophy. Hitler, Gandhi, Hannibal, Cromwell, Lenin—an ideological Tower of Babel, a multi-tiered political club sandwich. In due course the British put Nkrumah in jail, thus guaranteeing, as in the case of Nehru, that he would become prime minister and lunch with Queen Elizabeth in Buckingham Palace. As prime minister, still under British rule, Nkrumah broadcast an appeal to Ghana to "rise above its past"—above tribalism. He preferred "self-government with danger to servitude in tranquillity." Yet as the administrator of independent Ghana he wanted tranquillity. At the 1958 All-African People's Conference in Accra, over which Tom Mboya presided, Nkrumah, opposing the Egyptian and Algerian delegates, therefore advocated the quiet road of nonviolent revolution instead of the bloody way of the Mau Mau in Kenya. For the people, Gandhi; for himself, Lenin or Hitler or Mussolini or Cromwell.

Nkrumah, following Nehru, also favored "a modern socialistic pattern of society." But if, according to Nehru, the century-old theories of Marx and Lenin do not fit India, which is far superior culturally, technologically, economically, politically, and socially to any African state, they assuredly would be as incongruous south of the Sahara as a fur coat on a Zambesi fisherman. To African leaders, the appeal of socialism lies less in its economic program than in its dictatorial potential. Nkrumah has said, "Capitalism is too complicated a system for a newly independent nation. Hence the need for a socialist society. But even a system based on social justice and democratic constitution may need backing up, during the period following independence, by emergency measures of a totalitarian kind. Without discipline true freedom cannot survive." Neither does it survive totalitarian discipline.

Underdeveloped states are, by definition, short of capital in varying degrees. In Africa the degree is great. One method by which new governments can acquire capital is to confiscate foreign capitalist enterprises and deliver them into the hands of government bureaucrats for management. This is a broad highway to state capitalism. States as distant and different as Indonesia, Egypt, and Cuba have adopted this expedient, which kills two birds with one stone: it gets rid of the foreigner and pockets his property; it fosters xenophobic nationalism and state capitalism. That it helps the national economy or the people has yet to be proved. Unsympathetic outsiders thought Egyptians could not run the Suez Canal after Nasser seized it. They were wrong. But Congolese certainly could not manage the mines of Katanga. Fearing western capitalists arriving in imperialistic Trojan horses, African governments may, in their blindness and inexperience, bring in the superimperialists of the totalitarian East and lose their green independence. United Nations technical assistance has a big role to play here. Or the little neutrals—Switzerland, Sweden, Austria—could serve.

Within a few days of achieving independence and chaos, the Congo, larger than Western Europe yet inhabited by only 14 million people, was short of food, which had to be flown in from the United States, Adenauer Germany, Soviet Russia, and elsewhere. This is a measure of the unpreparedness and agricultural poverty. "Much African agriculture," the London *Economist* of December 13, 1958, wrote, "is caught in a circular dilemma—it cannot be more productive without greatly increased capital investment, but it cannot produce the capital until it becomes more productive." The dilemma is compounded by the family: the more productive a farmer becomes the more relatives appear to live off his bounty and devour his savings. (This happens in Asian cities and villages too.) Add the factor of illiteracy. According to a 1958 UNESCO survey, the percentage of illiteracy was 95 to 99 per cent in French Africa, 85 per cent in Tanganyika and Nigeria, and 70 to 80 per cent in Kenya and Ghana. African leaders will have to enlist unselfish foreign aid and be unselfish themselves. To clean Africa's Augean stables of the past requires hundreds of black and white Hercules. What an opportunity for idealistic American Negroes, Quakers, and individuals of good will everywhere! Advisers and practitioners are needed in all fields of endeavor: administration; education; sanitation; communications; preventive and therapeutic medicine for human beings and animals; mining; power development and industrialization; fishing and farming. The historic agricultural succession would be from tribal landholding to feudalism. This is not likely to be permitted

in the modern socialist-capitalist age. The new governments
are likely to grope for some form of cultivation intermediate
between peasant holdings and co-operatives, with the government engaging in export trade, of cocoa for instance, to
obtain revenue for government expenditures.

The first business of new governments, before they can
direct social revolutions or economic development schemes,
is to find the money to pay the salaries of the prime minister,
president, ministers, ambassadors, consuls, and clerks, and
the cost of office buildings, stationery, ink, cars, and the other
impedimenta of sovereignty. The government of Liberia
meets these obligations out of royalties from the Firestone
rubber interests and the Republic Steel Corporation's mining
operations. Ghana receives considerable income from the big
foreign concerns that take her cocoa and make it into
chocolate for the world's sweet tooth. When the British government announced in May, 1960, that Sierra Leone would
win freedom on April 27, 1961, it coupled the statement with
a promise of 7½ million pounds of spending money (dowry?)
for the departing daughter. This was wise and contrasts with
the French government's action when Sekou Touré, motivated by Marxism, or nationalism, or ambition, took Guinea
out of the French Community. In pique, the homeward-
bound colonialists carried off desks, chairs, typewriters, and
telephones from administrative offices and ripped out the
electric wiring. Other western powers, unwilling to provoke
de Gaulle's heroic ire, kept their hands in their pockets.
Thereupon, Sekou Touré held out his gray fur cap to the red
East, which responded with cars, contracts, cement, a printing
plant, and personnel. Frightened European and American
firms packed their bags.

Evidence piles up to prove that as long as the global cold
war lasts—and Peking and Moscow are energetically fostering
it—Africans, whether red or merely black, will find chinks in

the western armor through which to press spears tipped with blackmail. Often the attempts are clumsy. While the United Nations was landing troops in the Congo in the summer of 1960, Prime Minister Lumumba said, "If no action is taken by the United Nations, we will understand that the United Nations is a tool of imperialism—a plot of capitalists to grab the Congo." At that moment he had already requested Khrushchev to intervene militarily. The Soviet Chairman agreed with alacrity; he must have a full drawer of carbon copy promises to shoot rockets at offending "imperialists." But it is necessary to distinguish between a dog's bark and the bear's bite. The red Zeus hurling threat-thunderbolts, the red demagogue making black headlines, does not help his own country and hurts the colored and white peoples whom he appears to champion.

The roster of communist sins is long. They have wiped out millions of lives at home and suppressed and oppressed foreign nations. They have made the big-lie propaganda a world currency. But perhaps their worst crime is the sowing of hate. In our problem-ridden world, the ugliest is the color problem. The white and yellow communists spare no trick to aggravate and intensify it. For self-aggrandizement, for "the victory of socialism," they not only set nation against nation, they set race against race, color against color. Communism cannot be good when it deliberately spreads evil. Not much love is expected of governments. Not one drop of it resides in the heart of the Kremlin. Moscow and Peking, abetted by the little Moscovites and Pekinese, are peddlers of poison. Lenin's legacy to communists was: split. They accordingly chalked up an unrivaled record of splitting socialist movements, communist parties, countries, and continents—now the world. Is this their promised paradise?

Western nations, and the United States in particular, pour water on the communist mill by misrepresenting themselves.

The world, notably the underdeveloped, nonwhite world, is in a hurry. Revolution is the synonym of haste. Capitalism has become the synonym of congealed conservatism. Africans, like Asians, like Latins, prefer quick change and the power which they think goes with it. The powerless want power, hate the powerful, and applaud those, recently risen from weakness, who defy the most powerful, the United States, now identified with past domination by all whites. This may be the inversion of the photographic lens, the distortion of convex and concave mirrors, but it is through these glass devices, home-made or exported by communist states, that hundreds or millions see the West.

America, by misrepresenting herself, helps the communists to distort. If social revolution means rapid progress toward a classless society, toward reducing class differences by leveling lower classes upward, the United States in the past forty years has undergone a greater social revolution than the Soviet Union. If political revolution means the diffusion of political power once monopolized by one group, the United States, where there are now several power groups, including the trade unions, and many institutions that check and balance one another, has experienced an infinitely deeper political revolution in the past forty years than the Soviet Union, ruled by a tight oligarchy led by one person seen through the fog of a worshipful cult of personality. If technological revolution means mechanization and automation, the United States as a whole has climbed to the top of a high mountain range whereas Russia lives on high peaks (sputniks, jets, etc.) and in the primitive huts of wild gorges. In July, 1960, A. Kutuzov, chairman of the State Commission for Automation and Machine Building, reporting to the Communist Party's Central Committee plenum, revealed, according to Nora Beloff's dispatch from Moscow to the London *Observer* that "as much as 47% of the Soviet industrial labor force wa working by hand with no machines or mechanical aids." In agriculture, technology is even more retrograde. Most domestic cooking in the Soviet Union is done with wood or on single-burner kerosene primuses. If the economic revolution, as conceived by the socialist fathers, means the end of capitalist exploitation, the Roosevelt-Truman-Eisenhower welfare society has diminished it appreciably, whereas Soviet state capitalism has, for the glory of the state and dictatorship, driven it to Oriental extremes that would have horrified even the "robber barons" of the West in the nineteenth century.

Yet God forbid that U.S. propaganda agencies abroad call America revolutionary. The official American lexicon makes "revolution" a dirty word, and "welfare state" raises the hackles of swashbuckling congressmen sallying forth on asses to defend the obsolete. In this age of public relations, an art Americans are supposed to have invented and perfected, the United States consequently scores many zeros in Africa, Asia, and Latin America. A government may be its country's enemy. When misrepresentations are added to missteps, the result is distressing.

However, the United States, in conformity with its revolutionary origin—the first colony to win national independence —has consistently supported the liberation efforts of dependent territories. American pressure was the decisive factor in ousting Dutch power from Indonesia; nor has the United States attempted to substitute itself for Holland. President Roosevelt and others urged Winston Churchill, during the Second World War, to give freedom to India. All anticolonial movements in Asia, Africa, and Eastern Europe enjoy American sympathy. Even where, as in the Algerian question, American anti-imperialism threatens to alienate a sensitive ally whose membership in NATO, the keystone of the U.S. defense system, might be lost, there has never been any doubt about America's attitude. During the 1955-56 Suez crisis,

Secretary of State John Foster Dulles committed grievous errors and let France and England down so crudely that they, alas, considered themselves compelled to launch an ill-conceived, ill-prepared, ill-omened military expedition to the canal and the Nile. Everything the American head did was bad. But America's heart was in the right place: it felt that the attack on Egypt was an imperialistic throwback; it preferred principle to principal allies.

This does not make America immune to imperialistic throwbacks; witness Guatemala, where no basic solution was achieved through intervention. But if the United States be accused of imperialism in South Korea the answer is clear: without America's presence Russia or China would seize South Korea and impose an alien, totalitarian imperialism unwanted by the people, as Moscow has in the "people's democracies" of Eastern Europe. The Eisenhower administration, in fact, interfered so little in South Korea that Syngman Rhee flourished too long as a dictator. It was only when his regime became intolerably brutal that a paragraph spoken by Secretary of State Herter sent Mr. Rhee to Hawaii, where many more beautiful bungalows are available for little Caesars like Chiang Kai-shek.

Instinctively, though not always politically, Americans are on the side of the future—there is nothing else ahead—and the future spells, compels, anti-imperialism. France has learned this the hard way, first in Indo-China after a protracted, futile colonial war; now in Africa. The British, who hear Big Ben every evening, knew what time it was. If they had not discarded the Churchillian "hold our own" policy, India would today be worse than a hundred Algerias. But the French, noted for rationality, believed sentimentally that they could keep the hands of the clock pointing backward to the romantic period of empire. The sun and moon reputedly stood still for Joshua. They refused to obey de Gaulle. Time marched on. In fact it flew. In less than two years the French Empire vanished.

The process began in September, 1958, when President de Gaulle offered all fifteen French colonies the choice of independence or limited autonomy within a French Community—his own adored invention. Only Guinea, on Africa's Atlantic hump, chose independence. Paris, shocked, embittered, and disappointed, kept its promise. Indeed, de Gaulle seemed to be punishing Guinea by insisting on her secession. Yet far from acting as a warning, Guinea served as an example. For a while the other French African colonies were content with their new condition as members of the federal French Community; France retained control over the colonies' finances, defense, foreign relations, and many other services. Then, in September, 1959, the French Sudan and Senegal formed the Mali Federation (population 6 million) and asked for national independence and full sovereignty, but within the French Community. On June 10, 1960, the French National Assembly granted this request and, too, that of the island of Madagascar (population 5 million), renamed the Republic of Malagasy, for a similar status.

This development sired a more drastic one. Mr. Felix Houphouet Boigny, one of de Gaulle's earliest and most devoted supporters, had favored the federal French Community: limited self-government. He believed in tight ties between his own country, the rich Ivory Coast, and France. This, he felt, also suited other French African possessions. But when Mali and Magadascar won complete independence, he demanded more. Not to be outdone by them, he wanted total independence outside the French Community with the right, however, to negotiate a new relationship to the Community at some later date. Three other colonies—Dahomey, Niger, and Upper Volta—joined the Ivory Coast in an "entente" and took the same position. The "entente," a kind of bow and arrow around Ghana, got what they wanted on July 11, 1960. That very week, Gabon, on the west coast of Africa, just below the hump, achieved independence. The contagion then spread to Chad, the French Congo, Mauritania, and the Central African Republics. In effect, the French Community, conceived by de Gaulle as an intimate federal structure, a United States of France-Africa, had been converted into a loose Commonwealth resembling that of which Britain is the heart.

In the presence of this storm, General de Gaulle made his peace with it. He proved to be no Canute; he could not bid the tide of freedom recede. To refuse independence, he said, would have been "contradictory to our ideals." It would invite the world's disapproval and provoke interminable struggles "all for a benefit which would inevitably have melted away in our hands." France had to be realistic, he argued.

But then what about Algeria? If Gabon and Dahomey and Upper Volta and the Ivory Coast and all the others, why not more-developed Algeria? The official answer would be: Algeria was never a colony; it was always a part of metropolitan France, and its elected deputies sat in the French parliament in Paris. This is the formal aspect. The Algerians consider themselves a separate people and claim independence. It might be argued that the FLN, the Algerian National Front, has no mandate from all, or the majority of, the Algerian people. Perhaps, probably, not. How representative, however, were the leaders who successfully petitioned for the independence of Niger, Madagascar, and Gabon? Is France not engaged in Algeria in an interminable struggle all for a benefit which will inevitably melt away in her hands?

The presence of almost a million Frenchmen in Algeria is a serious complication. An accountant operating a computer might quickly calculate that it has cost France more to maintain half a million soldiers fighting in Algeria for six years than to transfer the million colons to France. The French economy could absorb them, especially if the Algerians in France chose to return to their own country once it had attained independence. All this would be extremely painful surgery. But not more painful than the prolongation of the war and the deterioration of France's world position.

The harrowing post-independence experience of the Belgian Congo may be a lesson to Africans and point to a solution in Algeria. The desire for independence is an irresistible wave which will, in time, submerge Portugal's colonies, Spain's enclaves, and Britain's remaining possessions. Or, as Prime Minister Macmillan put it early in 1960 in South Africa—one assumes he was not overlooking Kenya, Nyasaland, and Rhodesia: "The wind of change is blowing through the continent. The growth of national consciousness in Africa is a political fact, and we must accept it as such."

The acceptance of the inevitable by the European powers does not, however, release African nationalists from their obligations. Even independence is not an end. It should be a means to a better life, and if for a long period it leads to a worse life, as it has in some Asian countries, the nationalists deserve censure for allowing their emotions to banish their intelligence. Emotions, to be sure, dominate politics everywhere. Yet brains ought to retain some function. And the brains proclaim that after independence former colonies need help and must not close the door to it. The ideal solution would be an international agency to take independent yet underdeveloped countries by the hand and lead them to stability and prosperity. The UN may give birth to such an agency if it stays long enough in the Congo. Meanwhile, however, the newly free countries should not, in passionate intransigence and pathological suspicion, spurn the aid of their former "motherlands" or of other disinterested white nations.

Even with foreign aid, the present African generation can only begin to scratch the surface of the continent's problems. Dr. Reinhold Niebuhr, the distinguished Christian theologian and political liberal, writes: "Nothing that is worth doing can be achieved in our lifetime; therefore we must be saved by hope. Nothing which is true or beautiful or good makes complete sense in any immediate context of history; therefore we must be saved by faith. Nothing we do, however virtuous, can be accomplished alone; therefore we are saved by love." Africans, including Algerians, as well as Asians and Latins cannot do it alone. Therefore they can be saved only by love. The former "motherlands" and others should make it easier for the ex-colonies to love them, at least to like them and collaborate with them. But love is bilateral. Africans cannot take it into their heads that they are white—blameless—while everybody else is black—blameworthy. They should combat their own color prejudices instead of yielding to yearnings for revenge on past evildoers. Rebels should be conscious of the future else they will suffer in it. When Algerian rebels machine-gun Sunday picnickers on a beach or cut the throats of their own innocent peasants they commit crimes which do not help them today and will come home to roost tomorrow. Terror begets terror. The policy of an eye for an eye makes both sides blind. Those who give love will get it, and Africans need it. Mahatma Gandhi was the greatest colored man who ever lived. He liberated India through love and left a legacy of love to all men, black, brown, yellow, and white. I can imagine Gandhi saying to Mr. Lumumba or somebody else: "My friend, the fact that whites discriminated and even discriminate against blacks does not justify blacks in discriminating against whites." Color injustice and hysteria are poor instruments of government.

Black Apartheid is as bad as White Apartheid.

## chapter 11

# *Israel in Africa*

EUROPEAN nations, among them the Soviet Union, plus North America and the white members of the (British) Commonwealth are usually regarded as the sources of technical and material aid for the underdeveloped world. But at the opposite ends of Asia there are two nations, Japan, with 90 million inhabitants, and Israel, with 2 million, which possess trained personnel and technology to offer lagging countries. Japan, in addition, can export capital.

The memory of Japan's wartime depredations remains alive and obstructs international co-operation. But militarily she is no longer a world power and, given the Russian and Chinese strategic positions, Japan's posture is defensive, indeed increasingly neutralist. Even territories she invaded and enslaved have been inviting her economic assistance. Japanese, for instance, are constructing an oil refinery in Singapore. India too is increasingly receptive to men and machines from Nippon. A Japanese firm has signed a contract with the Indian government to help set up a watch factory. (To balance this public venture, a French company was permitted to enter into a similar relationship with a private Indian corporation.) Japan is importing two million tons of iron ore from India per year. Now a big Japanese steel combine will develop the iron deposits of the state of Madhya Pradesh, build a railroad there, and double India's iron ore exports to Japan by 1966, thereby giving the Indian government an appreciable increment of capital.

Diminutive Israel plays an interesting role in Africa and here and there in Asia. The dispersed Jewish people, born everywhere, born therefore to be cosmopolitan and universal, found no safe resting place amid the rising tide of nineteenth-twentieth century nationalism in Russia, Poland, and neighboring lands. The climax came when the most chauvinistic regimes in Europe, those of Hitler and Stalin, rose up to annihilate Jewry. The nazis melted down the bodies of six million Jews for soap. The Soviets undertook to destroy the Jewish personality and spirit, thus giving advance notice of what ultimately awaits the many nationalities of the Soviet Union. Today these minorities tenaciously cling to their culture; some even harbor separatistic ambitions. But with advancing industrialization and education, both inevitably borne by the Russian language, the ethnic minorities, constituting almost half the Soviet population, are doomed to slow cultural assimilation with the Great Russians.

The heirs of the biblical prophets, perhaps foreseeing the ominous writing on Europe's black wall, built themselves a perilous refuge on a coastal sliver of Asia. Their ancestors once lived there. But as a result of numerous peregrinations, the Israelis are Europeans in Asia. This is a major cause of their conflict with the Arabs. It also gives Israel a special function in retarded Africa. Israel is Europe without power and without territorial or other ambitions. Israel represents no danger to Ghana or Nigeria or Burma. Her aid therefore evokes no fear. Israel, moreover, has more than technology to export; she has experimented in socialism, and the experiments interest a growing body of Afro-Asians. Fate has made the world-wide people of the Book, the bank, and the shop the nationalistic agents to remote Buddhists, Hindus, and Christian-pagans of a modernizing social revolution which their Semitic neighbors resist.

The Ghana government owns 60 per cent, an Israeli private company 40 per cent of the Black Star steamship line operated by Israelis. After the first five years, Ghana may assume management and total ownership. Meanwhile, Israel has established a nautical training center, with Israeli instructors, in Ghana. Israel exports cement, tires, glass, ceramics, processed foods, pharmaceuticals, chemicals, paper, leather, and plastics to Ghana and buys cocoa, coffee, copra, manganese, hides, palm oil, and bauxite. The Ghana government owns 60 per cent, Solel Boneh (the capitalist department of Histadrut, the Israeli trade-union organization) 40 per cent of a corporation which erects public buildings and private homes in Ghana and trains Ghanaians in construction techniques. Israel sends professors to a Ghana college and gives scholarships to Ghanaian students in Israeli schools.

Meyer Brothers of Israel recently completed the biggest hotel in Monrovia, capital of Liberia. The Liberian Construction Company, an Israeli firm, builds roads and public works in Liberia. Israel is likewise building roads in the interior of Ethiopia.

Israel is also increasingly active in Nigerian economic development. In May, 1960, the minister of health of East Nigeria toured the hospitals of Israel. At the same time the East Nigerian minister of agriculture, Mr. P. N. Okeke, accompanied by Mr. N. A. Nwosu, the principal civil servant of the ministry, were on a fact-finding mission in Israel at the end of which they said, "There is a general awakening of recognition of Israel in the West Coast of Africa and we are glad that Israel makes her knowledge available."

On returning to Katmandu, his capital, after attending the world conference of scientists at the Weizmann Institute at Rehovot, Israel, Prime Minister B. P. Koirala of the remote Himalayan kingdom of Nepal announced that two Israeli technical delegations would visit his country.

When the post-independence time of troubles erupted in

the Congo, Israel immediately sent a first contingent of ten physicians plus supporting personnel (nurses, drivers, etc.) and medicines, medical instruments, and surgical paraphernalia.

Although all new Asian and African states are eager to industrialize, their central problem is agriculture. In this field, Israel presents a veritable laboratory of organizational forms: from big capitalist orchards, vineyards, and farms, to smallholder settlements, to villages co-operating in the use of machines and in marketing, to voluntary communes of the highest idealistic type. Fifty-six Burmese spent 1959 in Israeli co-operative villages and communes studying their methods. "Villages modeled on Israel's self-defense frontier communities are being set up in Burma," Tillman Durdin informed the *New York Times.* "During the beginning phase, several Israelis will be on hand to help." Like the Israelis on the Arab frontiers, so the Burmese on their long China border will be trained to farm and fight; they plow, plant, and reap with guns slung over their shoulders. "As an exporter of specialists and advisers," Durdin added, "Israel leads all other countries, while Israeli participation in Burmese business enterprises has shown a considerable increase. . . . Israel has brains and abilities for export, and by using Israeli experts, neutralist Burma can avoid turning to either of the two main 'cold war' antagonists, the United States and the Soviet Union, for specialists. Israeli experts, moreover, cost about half what would have to be paid to an American. . . . Israelis have advised the Burmese on the development of irrigation and methods of cultivation in the Central Burma dry zone, the raising of chickens, and the use of modern agricultural machinery. Israeli experts have developed strains of long-staple cotton and other crops suitable for Burma."

Africans likewise have availed themselves of the opportunity to learn and borrow. Ethiopians, Nigerians, Ghanaians, together with Thais, Ceylonese, Indians, and Burmese, sixty in all, convened in Israel in 1959-60 for a prolonged study conference. They represented governments, trade unions, co-operatives, universities, and social work and farm groups, and they moved from one type of farm to the other searching for the one best suited to their countries' requirements. They also investigated the role of Israeli trade unions as owners and operators of bus lines, factories, construction corporations, and retail and wholesale distribution networks. The Histadrut, helped by the AFL-CIO, has set up an Afro-Asian Institute in Israel where young Africans and Asians will train for leadership of trade unions and co-operatives.

"I have just returned from Israel with a very favorable impression about the rapid economic progress made by that small country as well as the significant advance made toward the achievement of a socialist society," wrote R. K. Patil in the August 19, 1959, issue of *Bhoodan,* the weekly magazine of Vinoba Bhave, India's walking saint. "Indeed, I carry the feeling that, in a socialist sense, it is one of the most advanced countries I know of. It has a mixed economy. Foreign capital is readily welcomed and is pouring into the country in an ample measure. And yet, barring a few exceptions, the differences between the largest gross wage or salary and the lowest would not be more than four to one. . . . About 70% of the economy is either in the public [state] or co-operative sector."

On the other hand, a piquant report in the daily Jerusalem *Post* on the extended sojourn of some Indian Gandhians in Israel contrasted their shy idealism with the raucous feuding among Israel's socialist groups. Nevertheless, Israel, as the world's closest approximation to a co-operative socialist commonwealth (laced with dark veins of religious intolerance, Judaic obscurantism, and extreme chauvinism) exercises a tremendous intellectual attraction on Afro-Asians with socialist aspirations.

Idealistic-ideological affinity apart, the unique relationship Israel has built up with her Afro-Asian friends is explained by their wish to avoid the rivalries, jealousies, and vapid "tools of imperialism" accusations that flow from accepting the aid of great powers. But when the front door is locked to the cold war it enters by the chimney and windows. The Arab countries, employing a vigor and stamina they need for their own development, continually hamper Israeli trade-and-aid contacts with Africa and Asia, and these efforts are abetted by Moscow and Peking and their underlings.

Though a peace-loving member of the United Nations, the United Arab Republic persistently advocates war against Israel. "I declare to the whole world," President Gamal Abdel Nasser said in Damascus—but he has said it a hundred times—"that we will regain our rights by ourselves and we will shed our blood, sacrifice our lives, including myself, ministers, and every citizen, for the realization of all Arab rights. Palestine must be liberated." As though answering yet doubting these bellicose proposals, King Hussein of Jordan asserted in Amman that his little land living on British bounty was ready to rally to the United Arab Republic if Cairo "is prepared to open a final battle against Israel, our common enemy." Ready to go to war or not, Nasser blocks the Suez Canal to ships touching Israeli ports, thereby embarrassing Israeli-African-Asian commerce, and is the guiding genius of a far-flung boycott of Israel so effective that even Nehru, who has established diplomatic relations with Franco Spain, refuses to do the same with Ben-Gurion's government. By contrast, Burmese Prime Minister U Nu, consistently courageous in condemning Russian suppression of the 1956 Hungarian nationalist revolt and Chinese aggression in Tibet, has visited Israel, exchanges ambassadors with Israel, and fosters cultural-technological ties with her.

The Arab countries and principalities can unite on the

commercial and diplomatic boycott of Israel; that brings in a visible though illusory profit. On the basic issue, however, Israel divides the Arab states. The death of Israel would cost Jordan its life. Now that Nasser's Egypt has absorbed Syria, the United Arab Republic wants to annex Jordan, which would then form the land bridge between the two unharmonized segments of the U.A.R. Cairo, accordingly, conducts a furious radio campaign against Hussein's little Jordan kingdom and is suspected in Amman of fomenting rebellion and instigating assassinations of Jordanian leaders. The disappearance of Jordan would make the U.A.R. an even more dangerous neighbor of Iraq than it is already. Whatever they say in public, therefore, Jordan and Iraq depend on Israel to save them from the voracious appetite of Nasser's nationalism.

In effect, the Arab-Israel duel masks Nasser's expansionist designs throughout the entire Arab and even the Moslem world. This would explain, among other phenomena, Tunisia's antagonism to Egypt and to the Egypt-dominated Arab League.

In sub-Saharan Africa, the Arab-Israeli conflict becomes enmeshed in a major religious-political phenomenon: the tendency of Islam to spread by conversions from the arid Moslem north to the verdant Christian-pagan south. Ghana is one of the new countries that feels menaced. Nigeria is divided. Chief Festus Okotie-Eboh, the finance minister of federal Nigeria, negotiated in Tel Aviv with the Israeli authorities for loans and export credits. The government of the North Nigerian state, largely Moslem, declared the acceptance of such assistance could be interpreted as "involvement in Middle East controversies; it would not accept any part of this aid." The independent *Nigerian Times,* in reply, wondered whether Northern Nigeria, "as a member state of the Federation, has a moral right publicly to dissociate itself from an agreement negotiated for, and on behalf of, the whole

Federation by the Federal Government." It added that dissensions over foreign policy would militate against the receipt
of "much-needed capital and investment from overseas." Another newspaper, the *West African Pilot,* organ of the National Council of Nigeria and the Cameroons, asked whether
it was "sound reasoning to hold that getting loans or credit
facilities from Israel by our Federal Government in order to
hasten our urgent economic developments is involvement in
the Arab-Israel conflict while hobnobbing with Arab digni-
taries all over the Middle East is not." The North Nigerian
position, it stated, was "funny and ridiculous." On September
24, 1960, Sir Abubakar Tafawa Balewa, Prime Minister of
Nigeria and a North Nigerian Moslem, announced the acceptance of an $8,400,000 seven-year loan from Israel although
President Nasser had reportedly urged Nigeria's fourteen
million Moslems to oppose the transaction.

Several African conferences have polarized toward Nkrumah and Nasser. To some extent this is a conflict of personali-
ties, to a greater extent a reflection of Black Africa's interests
clashing with those of Arab Africa. The rivalry occasionally
takes the form of a seemingly abstract debate on the virtues
of violence and nonviolence in which the Algerians and
Egyptians, backed by communists, glorify force and pagan
Christians advocate Gandhism, democracy, and parliamentary
politics. The January, 1960, All-African Conference held in
anti-Egypt Tunis, rebuffed an Egyptian-communist resolution hostile to Israel; so did the Positive Action for Peace and
Security in Africa convened in Accra in April, 1960. But the
same month, at the Afro-Asian Solidarity Conference in Con-
akry, Guinea's capital, the anti-Israel bloc, stiffened by delegates from communist countries, excluded Mr. Shlomo Hillel,
the Israeli ambassador to Guinea, from its sessions. In mid-
June, 1960, United Arab Republic Deputy Foreign Minister
Hussein Sabri told the Addis Ababa conference of African

tates that Israel was "a tool of imperialism . . . hiding behind a mask as a go-between for the colonial powers." He
added that African countries accepting financial assistance
from the big powers were "only tightening the colonial
stranglehold on Africa and will deter the full independence
of all Africa." One infers from this statement either that the
Soviet Union is not a big power or that the United Arab
Republic is tightening the colonial stranglehold on Africa.

There is not much use arguing with nationalism. To
foment Arab nationalism the Arab states are entitled to
boycott and otherwise molest Israel. As inmates of the world-
wide jungle of sovereignties, they have every right to arm for
the frequently and frankly avowed purpose of exterminating
Israel. Who can blame Russia for courting Cairo with credits?
One fact, however, is undeniable: The wealth of the Arab
sheikdoms along the Persian Gulf, of Saudi Arabia, and of
Iraq floats on oil; Egypt, Syria, and Lebanon earn considerable revenue from the transit of oil; but the future of Middle
East oil is unpredictable. Oil is already a glut on the world
market. Expanded production of Saharan and Libyan oil and
the probable expansion of Soviet oil exports will rob Middle
East oil of its crucial importance. In twenty or thirty or forty
years atomic energy will begin to make inroads on the use of
petroleum and gas. The Arab governments of the Middle
East have two, three, four, or five decades in which to lift up
their people from the present degrading poverty, disease, and
illiteracy to the threshold of civilized living. They would be
wise not to lose an hour of this time pulling Soviet chestnuts
out of the fire or undermining their economies by wasteful
preparations for war against Israel. That way lies decay and
death. The great powers—France, Russia, the United States,
and the United Kingdom—could help prevent trouble by
guaranteeing national frontiers in the Middle East and en-
forcing an embargo on arms shipments into the region. This

would not give the Soviets a status in the Middle East. They have it already.

Russia, even before the revolution, won a toehold in the Middle East through intrigues in Abyssinia, Egypt, Palestine, and Syria. At the United Nations the Soviet government voted for the creation of the Israeli state in order to get the British out and put an oar in. This is an old game in which the Arabs are pawns. So, by a turn of the diplomatic wheel, tiny Israel finds herself pitted, willy-nilly, against mammoth Russia. The two, totally different in almost every respect, have a certain lure for newly independent Afro-Asians. Both have successfully, speedily industrialized—to the regret, be it said, of some pioneer Zionists who conceived of their movement as back-to-the-soil cultural therapy—and both are called socialist though Russia's socialism is dictatorial state capitalism while Israel's is a democratic mixture of private enterprise and high and low forms of co-operative action, all voluntary.

The Israelis are Euro-Asians. They know the West and feel the East. They understand Afro-Asians because they understand the emotions released by suffering, persecution, inferiority, and frustrated hope. They combine western dynamism with their own peculiar idealism. They offer skills and goods to underdeveloped countries out of a wish to survive and serve. For former colonies that are not yet nations, Israel is a model of disparate elements welded into a purposeful union; Jews ingathered from two score countries, devout mystics and militant atheists, socialists of many hues, as well as orthodox and experimenting capitalists, quarrel and co-exist in a common, conscious effort to harness science and make a land of rock and sand flow with water and electricity, and some milk and honey. Israel is a school of nationalism and of socialism.

# chapter 12

# The Future of Communism

"SOCIALISM" is a plastic word which can be beaten into many shapes. It has assumed several colors: red, pink, gray, brown, and black. The communists call themselves socialists. Anticommunist British Labourites are called socialists. "Nazi" is a contraction of national socialist. Mussolini hailed the proletariat and worked at founding a corporate state for which he would have claimed the title of socialist. Nasser says, "We want to achieve a socialist, democratic, co-operative society." Nehru favors "a socialist pattern."

Socialism used to be dreams. When governments took it over it became a means, and meaningless unless married to adjectives and explanations. Socialism, once intimately related to freedom, internationalism, and the flowering of the individual, has become, in one third of the world, the equivalent of cannibalistic state power. In official Kremlinese and Pekinese, socialism is a phase, a way station on the road to communism. The difference between socialism and communism apparently consists in a sufficiency of consumers' goods. When the average Soviet citizen can buy as much for daily use as, say, the average north Italian, Athenian, or Frenchman, he will have entered the communist paradise. Communism is the terminus where evolution stops—according to Marx's ideological grandchildren.

This is nonsense. Evolution never stops. Communism will evolve and destroy itself.

The British Labour Party and the German Social Democratic Party, the two most powerful anticommunist socialist
parties in Europe, are today living through a grave crisis
that is relevant to the future of communism. It is a crisis of
prosperity.

At the Swiss lakes, on the French Riviera, on Spain's Costa
Brava, one encounters vacationing Cockneys, driving small
cars or scooters, whose fathers perhaps never left the slums
of London. At the funeral of Aneurin Bevan in his Welsh
constituency of Ebbw Vale, Mrs. Margaret Williams, chairman of the Rhymney Trades Council, said, "We come here
now in our smart clothes and our pretty hats, but it was
not like that when I first heard him speak up here in the
thirties." They would remember him, she declared, "as the
great man who stuck up for the poor."

The smart clothes, the pretty hats, the scooters, paid vaca-
tions, unpaid medical care, and other improvements were
the fruits of the social revolution which Bevan and his
Labour friends initiated and which the Conservatives pre-
served; it took the wind out of the sails of the Labour party's
economic program. To be sure, the class differences of which
D. H. Lawrence was so unalterably conscious, and the class
accents, remained. But Bevan's great gifts had lifted him
from pit boy to Whitehall, the upper class, and country
squiredom. A ladder stood waiting for others. Caste walls
were no longer unscalable. The B.B.C. was giving England
a national language. Above all, inherited poverty had ceased
to be a permanent badge. Black spots still dotted the map.
Ellen Wilkinson's Jarrow still glowered under the specter of
unemployment. But by and large the present and the prospect were brighter. Somehow the aftermath of the terrible
war had dissipated the material and spiritual gloom of the
1920's and 1930's. The party of the poor now needed a new
appeal to the not-so-poor, to the youths, who knew full em-

ployment and never the protracted unemployment of their parents, to the millions in new council housing, to the TV viewers, to car owners, to workingmen who aspired to be like the middle class, and to middle-class people who had property but did not feel close to the Tories.

Accordingly, Hugh Gaitskell, the Labour Party leader, a galaxy of bright young intellectuals concurring, proposed that Clause Four of the party constitution, which provides for the nationalization of private industries and utilities, be dropped overboard. It alienated the middle class, they argued, and meant nothing to new voters or to the workers who had climbed several rungs of the ladder that leads to security and prosperity. Nationalization of the Bank of England, coal mining, the railways, and so forth had made no broadly perceptible difference in Britain, and in Russia nationalization was the base of the dictatorship. Most persons whose lives are better would rather not experiment with such a device. To them the improvement in their condition is more important than what system or what men improved it. The thickness of the pay envelope eclipses ideology.

Nationalization, or the substitution of public for private ownership, had been the pillar of socialism. That the Socialist Party leader and a number of thoughtful Labour members of Parliament were ready to abandon it for government control, in some cases through government purchase of shares in private companies, reflected the smart clothes and the pretty hats: the new times. Nationalization, or Clause Four, became a battlefield between socialist revisionists and traditionalists.

German revisionism suffered no such birth pains. In West Germany, largely under the impact of material improvements similar to, perhaps relatively greater than, those in Great Britain, the socialists were routed by Adenauer in parliamentary elections on September 15, 1957. The defeated indulged in the usual marathon post-mortems. The 1959 Social

Democratic Party convention, by resolution, erased Marxism
and socialist ideology from its program.

Parties with millions of supporters like the German social
democrats and the British Labourites, as well as the French
and Italian communist parties, have a mighty momentum
which carries them through ideological vacuums. They are
often in office in cities and states—and power fortifies. They
cater to local interests and develop inner loyalties which sustain much of their strength. Moreover, the very citizen who
does not want them to tamper with the status quo looks to
them to defend his gains and prevent a deterioration. (In
France and Italy masses of communist voters would be horrified by a communist revolution yet regard the communist
parties as bulwarks against threatening reaction or fascism.)

Nevertheless, it is not enough to ride on inertia or to scrap
obsolete ideas. For its health and success, an opposition party
has to be able to grapple with the party in power on a big
issue that arouses popular passions and attracts wide attention. Fortunately for both the German Social Democratic
Party and British Labour, foreign affairs—including defense—
became a matter of life and death and purse just as economic
questions lost their political urgency and appeal.

The business of the opposition is opposition when profitable. It must try to offer an alternative policy. But the
attitude of socialists toward international politics is more
than a test of electoral drawing power. Foreign policy mirrors
their role in the nation. Are they of the nation or a class
apart?

After the First World War, the social democrats saved
Germany from communism and monarchist restoration and
might have saved it from Hitler had the communists not
stabbed them in the back and in the united front and split
the labor movement on Moscow's orders. Despite these
services to the nation, the socialists, thanks to their credo and

working-class membership and because the ruling class usually cold-shouldered, indeed brutally fought them, never were integrated with the German nation. This proved fatal to Germany. The Austrian working class, largely socialist-led, likewise felt isolated and treated almost as a foreign element in its own country.

In England, too, in very different circumstances, the working class in the 1920's and 1930's was deprived of the educational, economic, and political opportunities which would have enabled it to share the sweet sensations of national identification.

The Second World War weakened German nationalism, for Hitler, the national socialist, had been the father of national disaster. In England, on the contrary, it enormously strengthened national pride and cohesion. The Labour Party participated with effective patriotism as a full partner in Churchill's wartime coalition cabinet. Equality of sacrifice and service—lord and laborer fire-watched together through a thousand grim nights—gave the nation a supra-class unity. When hostilities ended, the Attlee Labour government performed a historic national function in taking England out of India and launching a second industrial revolution with creative welfare-state features which helped lift the country out of its prewar economic doldrums.

When, accordingly, the Labourites went into opposition in the 1950's and the cold war emerged as humanity's paramount problem, they encountered no difficulty in formulating a nationalist foreign policy. It was part of Aneurin Bevan's popularity not only with his own party but with the nation at large (and with many Tories) that as shadow, or heir apparent, foreign secretary he wanted a strong Britain equipped with her own hydrogen bombs and other military assets which would make his country the arbiter in world affairs. His pronounced anti-German sentiments and occa-

sional vehement criticism of America likewise endeared
him to nationalists, irrespective of party.

On this, as on nationalization, there was, however, no
unity in the Labour Party. The crushing defeat it suffered
in the 1959 elections at the hand of the Macmillan-led
Conservatives and the consequent prospect of four or five
long years without responsibility for governing the country
intensified the disunity. Gaitskell, weakened by the long illness and then the lamented death of Bevan, the most colorful
man in Parliament, would have consigned Clause Four to the
dusty archives and, in general, with deviations here and
there, followed the defense and foreign policies of the government. But the socialist traditionalists and the pacifist mili-
tants demurred. There had always been a strong pacifist block
in the Labour Party. The horror of nuclear war, the expense
of nuclear armaments, the inconvenience and possible em-
barrassment of semiautonomous American airbases in the
British Isles, and the emotional antagonism to the rearmament
of Germany reinforced the pacifist ranks. Appeasement, that
fateful disease of British diplomacy, raised its head in the
Labour Party. In some instances the very persons who
pilloried Prime Ministers Stanley Baldwin and Neville
Chamberlain for appeasing Hitler, Mussolini, and Franco
now advocated not only appeasement of Russia but Britain's
unilateral disarmament, the expulsion of American bases
and in effect, therefore, withdrawal from NATO. The chief
Soviet challenge, they contended, was social and economic
not military. To the extent that this was true, it resulted
from western organized military strength. What serious political leader could guarantee that if NATO were crippled
by the defection of England the Soviet challenge would not
become military? Who can promise that European military
weakness will not enable Russia to seize foreign territory
without war? The Soviet challenge is social, economic

and military. The challenge must and can be met on the three fronts. A defenseless, divided Europe might tempt Moscow, as a similar situation, which the Labourites then condemned, tempted Hitler, to start a war in the fatal illusion of quick victory. A rereading of Maxim Litvinov's speeches at the League of Nations and of the literary output of those brilliant Labourite pamphleteers who agreed with him might today be a salutary political exercise. To be sure, Hitler and Mussolini were fascists whereas Russia styles herself communist. But the name is tertiary to the facts. On the record, the Soviets have been aggressors, imperialists, and annexationists, and China quotes Lenin to justify war.

Some advocates of British unilateral nuclear disarmament exult in Soviet nuclear power. They can be dismissed as insincere. Some say Britain should increase her conventional armaments and leave nuclear armaments to America. They are not pacifists. Some contend that if Britain rejected nuclear arms Russia, America, and China would follow suit. They are naïve. There is no basis in fact or in logic for supposing that any country, even France, would forgo A- and H-bombs because England had done so. On the contrary, western weakness might stimulate eastern aggressiveness. Britain's military unpreparedness in the 1930's did not hinder Hitler, it encouraged him. But whom the gods wish to destroy they first make deaf to the cautionary lessons of history.

British Labour is caught on the piercing horns of a dilemma: either nationalistic isolationism and unarmed neutrality which, in practice, would be antinationalist; or, agreement with the Conservative foreign and defense policies, and what then of its role as an opposition party?

Was it by mere coincidence or the cruel logic of the situation that German socialists were faced with the same choice? After two world war defeats, masses of Germans had become deeply antimilitarist; West Germany, fervid anticommunism notwithstanding, would probably not have rearmed but for American pressure. Secondly, the German nation was painfully rent in two by the iron curtain and could not have peace of mind until reunified. The social democrats built a political platform by joining these two factors. If West Germany, they argued, were uncommitted, unaligned with the West, and unarmed, Russia would evacuate the Soviet zone in Germany and permit reunification. This gave every appearance of a popular, nationalistic policy that could garner votes when prosperity had robbed socialist economic ideas of their attraction. Kurt Schumacher, the remarkable leader of the German socialists, told me in Berlin in 1946 that, "If the Allies do not allow us to be socialistic we will be nationalistic." Not the Allies but the West German economic miracle after 1948 prevented his party from being socialist. Therefore it experimented in nationalism: national reunification through a foreign policy acceptable to the Kremlin.

On the other hand, Konrad Adenauer, the conservative octogenarian Catholic Chancellor, a man of a few simple principles which he followed with undeviating consistency, believed that Germany's salvation lay in intimate integration with the West. He stole the socialists' internationalism. Stubbornly, and even at the sacrifice of money and sovereignty, he promoted Franco-German amity to replace the enmity that spawned three man-eating wars in seventy years and split Europe. Steadily, he contributed bricks and mortar to the structure of a united Europe first of the Six, later of the Thirteen, eventually of the Twenty-two. I know from long conversations with him that he envisaged reunification as a consequence not of a bargain or barter, much less of a war, but of the mounting influence of a confederated Europe linked with America and armed through NATO plus, not least, social changes inside Russia which would turn her away from imperialism and thereby enable her to release the

Soviet zone in Germany for reunification with West Germany.

Year after year the steel-willed Chancellor and the Social Democratic Party remained locked in combat—and poles apart—over foreign policy issues. But some socialists began to waver. Slowly, more and more of them began to discern flaws in their interpretation of Soviet intentions. The Kremlin's frequent oratorical and paper avowals of coexistence might reflect the Soviet people's and even Khrushchev's wish for peace, but it was still coexistence for communist victory and had revealed no will to compromise on German reunification. A group of social democratic leaders who met the Soviet ambassador at his Bonn residence for a long heart-to-heart talk carried away the conviction that Moscow would not sanction reunification even if West Germany left NATO. Reunification was conditional on West Germany's going communist. That postponed it to the Greek calends.

Moreover, Russian insistence, after November, 1958, on West Berlin's becoming a "free city" meant not free in the sense of civil liberties but free of ties with the western powers and with West Germany, an isolated West Berlin, an island or ice floe rocking in the red sea that surrounded it and free to succumb gradually to myriad communist economic pinpricks, to vetoes on meetings to be held there, to obstruction of vehicles entering and leaving the city, and perhaps to civilian invasions from communist Germany. How would West Berlin, after the withdrawal of American, British and French troops in accordance with Soviet demands, cope with the intrusion of a hundred thousand or several hundred thousand rioting demonstrators from East Germany who behaved as the communist-socialist activists did in Tokyo on the eve of Eisenhower's scheduled (and descheduled) arrival?

Khrushchev's death blow to the unborn summit conference in May, 1960, had a perceptible impact on domestic politics in many countries—in Italy, the United States, Great

Britain, and most noticeably in West Germany, where socialist thinking on international affairs finally underwent a
radical change. The next month, the social democrats capitulated to Adenauer—threw in the sponge might be an
adequate description, for it had been a boxing match of
many rounds. The Social Democratic Party now proposed a
bipartisan foreign policy which they formulated in six points
that constituted a restatement of Adenauer's foreign policy.

But Adenauer, a prejudiced opponent of the social democrats in general, did not, in particular, forgive their adamant
hostility to his position in international politics. They had
fought him for years on joining the Coal and Steel Community, the Western European Union, the European Defense Community, and NATO. They had voted against the
creation of a West German army. Their acceptance of his
foreign policy no doubt delighted him, but he rebuffed their
collaboration. He would let them stew in their past mistakes.

To document their conversion, the Social Democratic
Party announced that in the impending federal elections,
Willy Brandt, mayor of West Berlin, would be their candidate for chancellor to succeed Adenauer. Brandt in his forties
had the advantage of youth over Adenauer in his eighties.
But the true significance of Brandt's nomination lay in the
fact that as commander in chief, so to speak, of the most
vulnerable and most decisive German and West European
sector of the anti-Soviet front, he had held West Berlin. He
thus became the symbol of national defense. While the Social
Democratic Party was creating an image of itself in the
public mind of soft appeasement, in an effort, to be sure, to
reunify Germany, he was performing a national function
by keeping West Berlin free. Of all outstanding socialists he
alone had discreetly yet firmly agreed with Adenauer on
German integration with Europe and on German rearmament. The Socialist Party was capitulating not only to Ade-

nauer but to its own Willy Brandt, the author, everybody knew, of the six points adumbrating the socialists' proposed bipartisan foreign policy.

Life had thus annulled the German Social Democratic Party's economic program and forced it into a liaison with Adenauer on his nationalist-internationalist foreign policy. In Austria, socialists were united with the Catholic Party in a long-lived coalition. Norway, under a labor government, regulated capitalist enterprises through price control and other means but did not hamper, much less persecute, private business. In British Labour, the alternative was Gait-skell without nationalization and with a Macmillan-like foreign policy or traditional socialism plus pacifist isolationism. Neither variant would worry the Conservatives. Japanese prosperity had induced the socialists to link forces with the communists for a nationalistic, pro-Soviet foreign policy.

What has happened to socialist parties reflects the twentieth century. Socialism as a popular political movement was a nineteenth-century attempt to solve the problems of poverty and exploitation created by the capitalist industrial revolution. In the developed countries—the United States and Canada, Western Europe, Japan, Australia, and New Zealand—poverty and exploitation are no longer major political issues. This is not to say that slums and other eyesores do not persist even in the richest western country, the United States, which has a serious unemployment situation that contrasts sharply with the scarcity of labor throughout Western Europe except Italy. Nevertheless, the high standard of living, the many welfare features like social security, unemployment insurance, state-aided housing, the medical care systems financed by the state or by voluntary contributions, the innumerable scholarships for higher education as well as the extension of compulsory education for precollege grades, and the general acceptance by all classes of these advantages as a social minimum have produced a condition which narrows the distinction between socialist and nonsocialist parties. The socialist parties may pride themselves on being responsible for this evolution, having prepared the ground for it by their propaganda and, in some countries, by their initiative when in office. The fact remains that in developed countries socialist parties and socialist governments have few special tasks that distinguish them from nonsocialist parties and governments.

This is what the twentieth century has wrought.

The developed nations of the world have now entered the twentieth century. Because of two world wars, the twentieth century arrived late. The date of its advent might be fixed somewhere about 1953 or 1954 or 1955. The problems of the twentieth century are not those of the nineteenth. Having filled man's stomach and put a better roof over his head, the wheels of a motorcycle, scooter, or car under him, and better clothes on him, and smart dresses and pretty hats on her, society is turning to new, twentieth-century business. A parent is now as concerned with the quality of TV programs for children as his grandfather was with the question of buying shoes for the family. A hundred years ago the urge was to get into the city and thereby raise one's living standards. Today it is to get out of the city and nearer the green countryside or suburbs. Social workers, psychologists, intellectuals, even politicians, are worried about the slow suicide of urban centers through overcrowding, inferior schools, juvenile delinquency, crime, noise, smoke, automotive gas fumes, the drudgery of work (in factory and farm) to which John Kenneth Galbraith refers, alcoholism—in socialist Sweden, capitalist France, and elsewhere—boredom, prostitution, and numerous similar metropolitan plagues. The primary consideration is no longer that of keeping body and soul together but of feeding the soul through the proper use of culture, leisure, and all the numerous conquests made by science and technology. Much as humanity has progressed, life is still quite backward compared to what one imagines it will be in the twenty-first century—if we survive. Survival by curbing war, hate, and violence is also high on the twentieth-century agenda. Mental illness follows on the next line; equality of rights and equality of opportunity in education and employment on the next; the husbanding of natural resources needs attention, and so also does waste in production, distribution, advertising, and government. Here is where socialists can find their new program. In the midst of these massive problems only the blind can be bored and no idealists will be without work, for man is just beginning to move toward the good life, and obstacles clutter the road.

The underdeveloped countries of the world, on the other hand, are still seeking their daily bread or rice, houses fit for human habitation, adequate changes of clothing, defense against disease, measures to prevent impoverishment through excess population, and political arrangements that will enhance man's freedom and dignity and forbid the exploitation of his body and mind by the state or individuals.

If one studies the affairs of underdeveloped countries, it becomes clear that their central goal is development. They wish to catch up with developed nations: Russia with America, China with England, India with the West. The underdeveloped regions—the Soviet Union, China, Asia as a whole, Africa, and Latin America—pin the banner of speedy industrialization to their mast. It is synonymous with socialism. Its dream is maximum capital construction—factories, railroads, dams; concern for the human cost is only slightly greater than was that of western capitalists when they were advancing through the long nineteenth century from underdevelopment to development. The socialism of today's underdeveloped world is no different in essence from the

capitalism of yesterday's western underdeveloped world ex
cept that when it is called communism it indulges in un
precedented exploitation and human humiliation.

Communism would be more impressive to those who seek
a better world if it were a way of life rather than a method
of production. But what, to the communist mind, deter
mines the nature of a social system is the pace of produc
tion. Thus Czechoslovakia recently began calling herself a
"socialist state" instead of "people's democracy" as theretо
fore, not because her inhabitants enjoyed more equality or
more freedom or had evolved a higher morality and lived
more co-operatively but only because her industrial output ex
ceeded that of the other people's democracies. Similarly, the
Soviet Union boasts of having achieved socialism and claim
to be marching toward communism on the ground that its in
dustrial production is greater. But if socialism had created a
new type of person we would know it and the communist
governments would shout it from the housetops. Khrushchev'
speeches, even at the UN, are heavy with production statistics
He avoids matters of the spirit. The study of philosophy in
the Soviet orbit is designed to raise factory productivity. The
result is that communism fails to conquer minds. The Hun
garian communist regime, after eleven years of educating it
youth, obviously had not won their hearts else tens of thou
sands of teenagers would not have fought the Soviet tank
in the 1956 nation-wide revolution. And the Soviet regime
in August, September, and October, 1960, in its forty-third
year, conducted a vehement campaign day after day in the
pages of the authoritative *Pravda* under the slogan, "Who
does not work shall not eat," against idlers, shirkers, "de
bauchers," and speculators "especially among the youth."
The ugly battle to survive and the hard struggle to succeed
have bred a crass materialism that does not produce a noble
human being. Nevertheless, there is evidence even in Soviet

literature that the Soviet system has not perverted the Russian character. Socialism in communist countries is a surface phenomenon, a form of organization, not a way of life, and future generations, rejecting the cruel, tense past (as Khrushchev, in part, rejected Stalin), will transform it, alter it to soften and sweeten its effects, make it less competitive, less fatiguing for body and soul, more conducive to decency, honesty, and friendliness. Compulsion will abate and the individual will not be sacrificed, as now, to the Moloch of the party-state. Russia, with her long strides in modernization and with her immensely talented people, may be the first to graduate from the nineteenth century into the twentieth. Other underdeveloped countries, whether socialist or capitalist or socialist-capitalist, will follow suit. Then names like socialism, communism, and capitalism will lose their meaning for them as well as for the West, and socialist and capitalist parties may die, and men will join together or clash depending on their attitudes toward the purpose of life and how it can best be achieved. Creative minds should address themselves to the quickest possible elimination of nineteenth-century vestiges at home and abroad and to discovering the art of twentieth-century living. In it, the development of man will take precedence over the development of countries and the striving for individual excellence will altogether eclipse the drive for national power. Human ingenuity will then face a challenge on two levels: the international, where nations, instead of competing for victory at the expense of others, shall collaborate in friendship for mutual benefit; and the personal, where man, working alone or in groups, shall serve others and thereby himself.

## chapter 13

# A Foreign Policy for America

POLICY is the composite result of national history, varied interests, opportunities, and possibilities. All these factors are refracted through persons. Men make policies, and the men should be the right ones. In the current crisis, the United States needs a Special Secretary of State for Africa, a Special Secretary of State for Asia, and a Special Secretary of State for Latin America, each one of whom is distinguished by a big brain, warm heart, broad vision, and color blindness. If they cannot be found in the bureaucracy or in law offices, the search should be extended to other domains. America is rich in talent. The Secretary of State, the co-ordinator of the activities of the Special Secretaries and of the entire Department of State, must be a mellow statesman whose chief task is to sit still and think and plan. His equipment will include a perspective of history, a deep human sensibility, an understanding of the laws and the limits of power, a constant awareness of the influence of changing technology on world politics, a grasp of the revolutions of our time, and a wide, clear-eyed view of what is happening in Russia and in China and how their challenge can be met in a way that helps them evolve and preserves world peace.

What does Russia want? Russia, like China, wants what nations have wanted in centuries past: to hold what she has and to get more. The expansion of power and territory has always been regarded as essential to the protection of the homeland and its earlier gains. Great Britain, for instance, believed that the maintenance and expansion of her empire were prerequisites of her material well-being and military defense. Today that empire has dwindled to insignificance and is still dwindling. Some families suffered. Yet the bulk of the population enjoys the highest standard of living ever, and alliances provide England with more security than she would have had through her own strength.

Immediately after the Second World War the British people broke open the door to the twentieth century. In 1947, by liberating India, they crossed the threshold. Now they have entered an era whose chief characteristic is the desire to live well. As a nation England wants nothing beyond influence to keep the world at peace. The domestic dispute is about how to do it.

The United States was never a feudal country. Capitalist development began early, especially after the hurdle of slavery had been destroyed by the Civil War, and moved quickly through a period of "robber baron" exploitation to wealth unknown in history. President Franklin D. Roosevelt's New Deal, beginning 1933, transformed unalloyed capitalism into a welfare state; government, trade unions, public opinion, social organizations, and the capitalists' sense of what was good for them have combined to establish a system of curbs, controls, state subsidies, and self-restraint that has enhanced personal and corporate security and resulted, come boom, depression, or high water, in unprecedented mass opulence and in something which even Marxists recognize as an approximation to the classless society. The majority of Americans want more of the same. The majority of humanity, communists included, pay America the compliment of aiming to catch up with her.

Those to whom private enterprise and free competition were a religion would revolve in their graves if they knew today's America of billion-dollar supports for industries, home builders, road builders, farmers, and foreigners, and official intervention in a thousand economic situations. Nor does the United States conform to the Leninist and non-Leninist orthodox concepts of a capitalism which must grow a superstructure of imperialism. Having great spaces and resources, having no neighbors to worry them, Americans never grew restlessly nationalistic and therefore imperialistic. The country preferred to stay at home in isolationism. Except for a brief period after 1898, Washington spurned overseas possessions. To prevent the victory of a nation that might subsequently menace her, America fought in the First World War and then withdrew from the scene asking no recompense for sacrifices made. Had it not been for Soviet Russia's threat to Europe after 1945, history might have repeated itself.

Even today, with an American foot or finger in many lands, most Americans would gladly revert to their prehistoric phase of nonalignment and nonparticipation, and concentrate on amassing more material comforts, luxuries, and dispensable gadgets.

This desirelessness is at once the strength and the weakness of America's foreign policy. It gives Americans a feeling of self-righteousness and generosity and the conviction that since they do not covet territory or power for power's sake the world will ultimately take the same view. The Marshall Plan billions gave the United States no power over Europe, and as real estate South Korea was not worth the price; but the prevention of World War Three was. Americans believe firmly that their far-flung alliances and foreign interventions serve the defense of self and everybody else against the dragon of communist imperialism. If it were not for this they would retire into their interoceanic redoubt.

Reluctant America needs to be aroused by a sense of crusading. Eisenhower called his book about the Second World War, *Crusade in Europe*. It is the faith in their idealistic crusade for a just cause that enables Americans to shoulder the heavy burden of their foreign policy.

The suspicions of foreign cynics and critics, therefore, cause bitterness. Moreover, desirelessness, whether only subjective or also objective, is a handicap. To want a thing passionately is to behave decisively. But after communist expansion had been blocked in Europe and Korea, desirelessness set in and initiative vanished. American foreign policy became defensive trench warfare designed to meet the adversary's manifold maneuvers on a zigzagging front that encircled the globe several times.

Trench warfare in the First World War was terribly expensive in lives, time, and treasure. In the Second World War, the nazis outflanked France's Maginot Line and roamed at will. It is not very different in current diplomacy. Khrushchev vaulted over the trenches into Egypt, into Cuba, and sent flying wedges to all five continents. Digging in is a necessary but limited and insufficient operation.

There is a widely held view that if Stalin had expected the United States to fight for South Korea the war would not have erupted. But the withdrawal of all American troops from the lower half of the peninsula and the absence of an unmistakable statement of America's intention to defend the area brought on the catastrophe. Everybody (the UN armies, Russia, and China) paid dearly for uncertainty. The adversary, whose caution exceeds his combativeness, might be grateful in the future for bright STOP signs.

No one would like to step onto a hydrogen-bomb or atom-bomb minefield. Do NOT ENTER signs, DO NOT TOUCH signs prevent everybody from getting hurt. The STOP markers around West Berlin are there in accordance with a 1944 treaty ratified by the Soviet government. If the men of Moscow believe in peaceful competitive coexistence and in the superiority of their social system they can try to prove it in the city of Berlin, where communism and the West can be seen from the same street corner.

Except for socialist Sweden, socialist-Catholic Austria, and communistic Yugoslavia, the untouchable line between NATO and the Soviet bloc is already clearly demarcated, and few will doubt that if any of these three neutrals were attacked the West, on request, would resist.

Europe's NATO members, however, have a grievance against the United States. The Pentagon recognizes the necessity of nuclear weapons for European defense. They have been stored in Europe. But the U.S. administration has refused to place them under NATO control; it retains the control. This reflects distrust, creates distrust, and undermines the alliance. Until nuclear disarmament, the equipment of NATO with A- and H-bombs would guard individual countries from bankrupting themselves by manufacturing them nationally, conduce to European cohesion, and remove a cause of considerable irritation between Europe and America.

The Kremlin still thinks it can disrupt NATO. The indications are Khrushchev's maneuvers to detach France from Germany, his push against West Berlin, his repeated diatribes against West German "militarism and revanchism," and his warnings to Norway, Denmark, Greece, Italy, and other NATO members not to permit missile launching pads on their territories. Khrushchev hoped to neutralize Italy and detach her from NATO and was disillusioned and angry when President Gronchi's visit to Moscow did not produce that result. If Moscow tries again and fails, the lesson cannot but reach the brain. Greater European unity and the Soviets' acceptance of it as a fact will lead to relaxation of tensions. This is a crazy world with a reserve of sanity. Only when both sides know they can get nowhere will they proceed from diplomatic fencing to fruitful talks with a view to arms limitation and a settlement in Europe that may release some nations from bondage.

Disarmament has been on everybody's tongue but in nobody's mind. When any country has disarmed unilaterally or by bilateral or multilateral agreement it can throw the first stone at the glass arsenals of others. The argument about which comes first, disarmament or trust and security, is as old as the chicken-and-egg conundrum. At the moment, tensions and inventions inhibit disarmament. "All that is possible," writes editor-in-chief Eugene Rabinowitch in the September, 1960, *Bulletin of the Atomic Scientists,* a monthly magazine reflecting the physicists' sense of guilt and their humanism, "is to try to slow down this competition by partial disarmament, or at least a partial cessation of weapons tests. Even this is difficult, and the progress is bound to be slow, because the mutual interest is purely negative, and overshadowed by the overwhelming and fully legitimate interest in not falling behind in the arms race." The end of the ice age will dawn when the Soviet and American economies begin to creak and Europe, united, is strong in conventional arms. Meanwhile there is no alternative to holding the line.

But the situation in Latin America, Asia, and Africa is so different from Europe's that STOP signs on a line of demarcation cannot be envisaged. Many countries in those continents say they are not asking to be defended.

For the formulation of a wise American, and western, policy toward Latin America, Asia, and Africa one thing, above all, is required: a deep understanding of the nature and use of power. Today power is not what it used to be.

In the London *Times* of August 13, 1960, the Tokyo correspondent of that newspaper told a tale out of Japan's past. "In 1862," he wrote, "a Shanghai merchant named Richardson, and two other Englishmen, attempted to cross the imposing procession of Prince Saburo Shimadsu, the father of the lord of Satsuma, as he returned from Edo, the capital, accompanied by an escort of some 400 retainers. To interfere with such a progress was a gross affront, and Richardson was cut down by the samurai in the daimyo's suite, and the other two wounded.

"The British government demanded of Edo an apology and an indemnity of one hundred thousand pounds sterling, as well as the execution of the culprits and a further twenty-five thousand pounds sterling from Satsuma, which the Shogunal government was powerless to enforce. The following year, a British squadron of seven men of war anchored in Kagoshima Bay, and, on refusal of repeated demands, bombarded Kagoshima, destroying a battery and setting fire to the northern part of the city. The people of Kagoshima decided that discretion was the better part of valor, and negotiations ended in an amicable settlement." That was power, naked and bare of scruples. The correspondent adds a delightful touch in his next sentence: "The action left no bitterness, rather the opposite." A sweet taste of powder, apparently.

Those were the days of power and faith in power. Today the United States has infinitely more power than it or any country possessed in the past. But little Cuba defies mighty Uncle Sam across a narrow strait just as Mexico did some years ago when she nationalized American and British oil properties.

We live in an upside-down, double-standard world. Within their iron curtains, Russia bathes Hungary in blood and China liquidates Tibetans and Tibet. Outside, both pose as champions of the oppressed. Castro cries "American imperialism" and "aggressor" while he confiscates American investments. Peking and Moscow approve, applaud, assist. Then Eisenhower, in angry retaliation, withdraws the U.S.

Cuban sugar subsidy. Whereupon the Latins say, "You did it because Fidel seized the refineries of American oil companies. Your foreign policy is dictated by big capital." A new government rises in Laos and declares itself neutralist. In response, a member of the House of Representatives announces that economic aid to Laos must be re-examined. "Ah," Asia retorts, "you use economic help to buy military allies. You are not interested in the welfare of people."

Not only is gunboat diplomacy out. Even dollar diplomacy no longer works. In the European trench power deters. Elsewhere power is powerless. When the United States gives guns and gold it is denounced. When it withholds them it is resented. Why?

The State Department recruits economic experts and legal experts. It should also have a corps of psychologists acquainted with the mentality of the underdog and his relation to power. Nothing gives the liberated slave more pleasure than heaping scorn on a former master. Playing David to Goliath is a congenial role for any leader aching to become a hero in the eyes of his people. It would be unnatural for the poor and weak to "turn the searchlight inward"; they regard themselves as the innocent victims of power wielded, usually, by white powers. True, America never had colonies in Africa. But the Congolese, incited and excited by Lumumba's demagogic oratory, slapped Canadians, beat Americans and spat at Norwegians. All whites were Belgians to them. In India every white person is a "European" though he be a fourth-generation Texan. Of course, Russians too are white. But, whereas the United States is the ally of the former European colonial nations, the Soviet government is their critical opponent, and Marx's mantle and the Lenin look still conceal Kremlin imperialism. Or the cynics boldly use Russia to blackmail America. If their bluff is called, Russia, an expanding exporter and importer, delivers the goods—to Egypt, to Cuba—and thereby encourages renewed defiance of the United States. The subtler governments take help from one side in order to get more from the other side and hope that the first will outbid the second and the second the first and so on ad infinitum. They need all the assistance obtainable. They feel more assured in their economic and political independence if they do not depend on one country or one camp.

Russia and China offer themselves as the alternative, the alternative to the dark past. In the post-mortem debate in the Belgian Chamber on the Congo, Minister of African Affairs de Schryver confessed: "The decolonization was insufficient for many years. We should have commenced the Africanization of the administration years ago. We should have started it ten years ago. We are all responsible for this." A Dutch statesman might make a similar statement in regard to Indonesia. Someday a Portuguese minister may express the same regrets. The communist nations have only to underline well-known facts.

In Nigeria, independent after October 1, 1960, 50 per cent of all children die before they reach the age of five. An African mother's tears for her dead baby are no different from those of the Massachusetts or Manchester mother, and in blind fury she curses the condition that killed her child. The status quo is unloved. Quick change is trumps. Self-advertising makes communists the agents of revolutionary innovations.

What a long leap for Khrushchev from the Kremlin battlements to the arms of Castro, right under the beard of Uncle Sam! The past prepared the way. Washington was the friend of Batista, as it was the friend of Stalin and Syngman Rhee and Menderes, as it is the friend of Franco and other dictators who destroyed democracies. What else could one expect? America cannot go round the world interfering in domestic politics to overthrow despots. It could of course refuse help. It did that with Nasser and drove him to Moscow. Though Nasser keeps communists in concentration camps, the Soviets put out the big red carpet and a welcome mat. There is room in Moscow for all sorts of dictators and democrats; there was room for Hitler's man Friday, Ribbentrop. Washington offers the same indiscriminate hospitality. It received Khrushchev. Peals of thunder would have rolled out of all the heavens had the door been shut in his face. The guiding principle of international politics is to be unprincipled in the interest of peace and friendly relations. So American politics held the hand of Batista while he was fighting Castro. It would have embraced Castro after he defeated Batista. In fact, the Eisenhower administration tried; there was at least no hostility, and the big sugar subsidy remained. Fidel pledged loyalty to democracy. He had a good press in the United States. He received an ovation in New York and cordial receptions in Washington. Then began the executions. Six hundred were executed, Françoise Sagan subsequently reported to the Paris *Express* from Havana, most of them condemned at open-air mass meetings ordered by Castro and all of them, she assures, recognized by witnesses as torturers and assassins. Two Rosenbergs and one Chessman, after exhausting the numerous legal devices and delays, were executed—unnecessarily, unwisely—in the United States, and how loud the outcry! But Castro was a revolutionist. You cannot make an omelet without breaking heads. Violence begets violence. The murder of enemies multiplies enemies. Castro cracked down. American criticism irked him. He began to attack the United States. The communists supported him as they had supported Batista till he suppressed them, as they had supported Perón in Argentina. Communists infiltrated the Havana government.

It is important to remember, however, that Castro won his

victory without communist support. He started alone as the apostle of the poor, the evangelist of land reform, the prophet of nationalism. The confiscation of big estates held by American companies, the attempt at escape from almost total economic dependence on the United States, the commitment to a higher living standard—all these flowed from his initial, essential role of liberator. To be sure, he made a million mistakes. He was a silver orator but a wooden administrator. The communists laid traps for him and he fell in. He exchanged the dollar's grip for the bear's hug. The island rocked in a turbulent sea of troubles. Nevertheless, Castro was the natural, legitimate son of his country's need to break with the past, with poverty and dependence on the foreigner.

Cuba and the Congo are comparable examples of bad timing, of no sense of time. The Belgian minister admitted that Africanization should have commenced ten years earlier in order to give the colony a decade's apprenticeship in self-administration before independence. Belgium failed to anticipate the storm, did not see the barometer falling throughout the underdeveloped world. When India and Pakistan became independent in August, 1947, Holland, France, Belgium, and Portugal should have known that the bell was tolling for them too. The hour had come to decolonize, to prepare Africa and Asia for freedom. And the United States, always the champion of anticolonialism, should have heard the knell and begun to lay the foundations of Latin-American economic independence. After Castro had torn a rent in the fabric of U.S.-Latin relationships, Washington hurriedly sewed on a $600 million patch. But a stitch in time . . . an ounce of prevention . . . vision, prevision, imagination. The President of the United States should have a weatherman always at his elbow. Secretary of State George C. Marshall was a good political weatherman. Suppose the Marshall Plan had been delayed till 1958?

To tell the time is to foretell the weather. The time to have dealt with Castro was before he had ever been heard of, and it would not have been necessary to overthrow Batista with U.S. Marines. The Japanese typhoon that swept away the Eisenhower visit in 1960 had been raging, with regularity, since 1952, and was duly noted on many weather charts. In these circumstances crude pressure for a U.S.-Japanese defense treaty was certain to bring an explosion. After visiting Turkey in 1952, I wrote about "a reaction against democracy and a retreat into the past. Religious reactionaries were being used [by politicians] to speed the retreat . . . Menderes and other leaders of his Democratic party resented newspaper criticism, placed critical journalists and opposition leaders under arrest." These were the causes of Menderes' overthrow in 1960 by the army and intellectuals. "The Turks," I had hinted years earlier, "are sensitive to what other countries, particularly France and the United States, think of them." No bludgeons were needed. Syngman Rhee might have occupied that Hawaiian villa five years before he did. There are ways, if there is a will, to give a new direction to Spain.

It is not a matter, therefore, of being reconciled to a regime, even one hostile to freedom, because America cannot allow the development of a power vacuum at any crucial point in its line of defense. A power vacuum has developed in Cuba as a result of U.S. support of Batista. Power vacuums may develop in Asia, Africa, and Latin America where no American military line of defense is possible. It is in these continents that bad timing, the lack of insight and foresight, takes a toll. They are the angry continents of the poor, the defeated, and the weak.

Rightly or wrongly, the needy impose a duty on the wealthy. And what hurts as much as poverty is inequality.

Americans worked for their present benefits. Yet the abundance they enjoy creates envy which sours to hate. Then a Castro finds admirers from the Rio Grande to Patagonia.

Sometimes Russia's foreign victories are puzzling. Actually, they have not been numerous except when her armies marched during the Second World War. Yet her successes seem spectacular and many wonder why. One reason is that hatred is a cheaper commodity to sell than moderation or love. Moreover, the incendiary's job is quick and easy. A match and a rag dipped in kerosene set fire to a building erected after months of toil. But when the chips are down, construction pays better than arson. Available documents prove that in 1948 Moscow ordered insurrections in Malaya and Burma; they continued for years after it had been clearly demonstrated that their only possible achievement would be additional misery for the miserable masses whose cause the communists allegedly championed. The Kremlin men have grown wiser and so have their minions abroad. Yet the will to divide, disrupt, and obstruct still persists. Witness Soviet policy in two major danger areas:

India is nonaligned. Secretary of State John Foster Dulles was, until he saw the light, intolerant of neutralism. The Soviet communists, at first, regarded Gandhi and Nehru as tools of imperialism and India, even after independence, as a British colony. Then they understood the advantages of neutralism and courted Nehru. Meanwhile, the United States armed its ally, Pakistan. This made India sentimentally anti-American and pro-Soviet. Moscow, accordingly, sided with India in the Kashmir issue. Khrushchev and Bulganin went to India and said that all of Kashmir should be India's, not Pakistan's. This was balm to Indians and widened the breach between the brother-countries of the subcontinent. The West, through the World Bank, spent a decade in patient negotiations—most of them conducted by

Mr. W. Iliff of Great Britain—and finally succeeded in getting an Indo-Pakistan agreement to a billion-dollar, ten-year Indus Valley water scheme with a view to healing the breach and lowering the temperature of the Kashmir dispute. The scheme ties severed arteries together again. It is a curative, creative, positive contribution to Asian peace.

Similarly, the United States offered a Jordan Valley development plan to bring Arabs and Jews together through the common use of precious water for their thirsty lands. Eric Johnston, the American negotiator, foundered on the rock of Arab intransigence. Subsequently, the Soviet Union undertook to build the High Dam for Egypt but it has not, to say the least, used the influence gained through this and through arms deliveries to dissuade Nasser from inciting Arabs against Israelis, to the economic and political detriment of both.

The moral is: Keep trying to build buildings and bridges. The architects of American foreign policy have several models: Marshall Plan, Indus Valley scheme, etc., which they can adapt to the contour of the land, the character of the people, and the conditions of the country or countries. Africa's first need is probably giant fertilizer factories. In most of the less-developed world solar energy has to be harnessed; in most of it sea water needs to be desalinated for drinking and farming purposes. All such enterprises are best financed and managed by international institutions like the World Bank, hardheaded, efficient, nonpolitical. As often as possible, Moscow should receive an invitation to join. Someday the Soviet rulers will find co-operation less expensive and nerve-racking than competition.

Before anything else, and more than money, the underdeveloped countries require trained personnel for administration, sanitation, education, modernization, family planning. (Eight out of every ten babies born in Sierra Leone die before they are one year old. If the eight were not conceived at all, it would be better for mothers and others.)

New states can borrow trained personnel. A British admiral commanded India's navy for eleven years after independence. Nkrumah kept many British officers in Ghana's armed forces. Stalin employed scores of American, British, and German technicians far into the 1930's. Foreign experts work and simultaneously prepare their replacements. Sooner or later nationals must take over from outsiders. If no facilities are available at home they can be educated abroad. But whenever feasible it is better for underdeveloped countries to import teachers than to export students. Indonesia in 1958 had contracts with the University of Kentucky, the University of California, and Tuskegee Institute to supply textbooks, laboratory equipment, and faculty for several of her colleges. The United States should have a Teachers Bank or a Science and Technology Bank where developing countries can make loans at no or low interest.

An intelligent American foreign policy will give priority to a vast training program for underdeveloped countries. This may sound prosaic but it actually has all the poetry and importance of the baby beginning to walk and of the adolescent growing to maturity. With the training of specialists should go the inculcation of the habit and respect for work. General Gursel who led the 1960 Turkish revolution and President Ayub Khan of Pakistan have recently stressed the need to work harder. A realization of the dignity of labor in countries where white collars and clean, uncalloused hands are the mark of high status would be worth hundreds of millions of dollars. The greatest unused asset of underdeveloped countries is their labor. This is their capital and if they put it to work they would require less foreign capital. Considerable loans and credits will, of course, still be necessary. These should be given for specific construction or development projects—not to balance the budget—and preferably from bank to bank, even though on both sides the banks are state-controlled. Governments tend to waste money out of political considerations.

Bigger funds would be available for economic development in Latin America, Africa, and Asia if the United States gave them less in military aid. Outside of NATO there is little justification of military allocations to foreign countries. Latin America and Africa ought to get no military support. It only makes for dictatorship at home and mischief with neighbors.

All aid programs are, in their very nature, international and would promote internationalism if so motivated. Colored skins are thin skins. Weak, newly independent countries as well as weak old countries labor under the handicap of extreme sensitivity, colossal pride, and numerous suspicions. The finest American impulse to help generates in the recipient a fear rooted in helplessness or sad experiences. To deal with this is the job of a psychologist working on the American mind. Some Americans resent the fact that they do not get bases, allies, friends, and voting support in the UN in return for the $60 billion they have given away since the Second World War. But this kind of profit motive defeats its aim. The purpose of American assistance should be to help countries help themselves. That was the great achievement of the Marshall Plan. America ought to ask no other reward. In fact, this is actually the greatest reward. The goal is a stronger, therefore freer, therefore better world in peace. Why, then, pin the Stars and Stripes to aid? People dislike the self-advertising and self-seeking and sometimes bite the hand that feeds them just to prove that they are not beholden. It happens in relations between individuals too.

Wherever practical, therefore, American aid can be dispensed through the World Health Organization, UNESCO, the UN Special Fund, UN Technical Aid, the Southeast Asia Colombo Plan, the Organization of American States, or similar aggregates of countries. Co-ordination should be the first law of foreign aid. If it is found, for instance, that several neighboring African countries have the same problem which is best handled across national frontiers, America should urge them to co-ordinate their activities and then place its resources at the disposal of a central authority. This may contribute to African regional or continental unity or at least moderate the dissensions which, despite pious obeisances to "the mystic of Negritude" and verbal commitments to Pan-Africa, split the Mali Federation before it was two months old and divided the micro-nationalisms of the sub-Saharan domain—sometimes about frontiers inherited from the colonial age of arbitrary map carving.

Modern man, and especially the modern statesman, will take a broad view of internationalism. There is no doubt that the international organization which implemented the Marshall Plan inaugurated the current progress toward European unity, stability, high prosperity, and security. It seems that in cold war conditions international co-operation spells safety for democracy. Perhaps this is why China and Russia oppose it. A free America in a freer world needs a more perfect union or unions whose size is limited by considerations of efficiency, not of narrow-minded traditionalism.

To give greater effectiveness to a new American foreign policy will be a protracted business, yet the urgent business of peacemakers and liberty lovers. The demagogue with the instantaneous cure, the adventurer proposing magic surgery, the merchant of hate selling hate is a liability. A quick presidential or cabinet-member visit, a brief summit conference, a single speech, accomplishes little. Indeed, progress toward world peace and freedom is a far more protracted, complicated business than the formulation and implementation of a wise foreign policy. Success abroad depends on material and spiritual strength at home.

America's economic system is a mighty one. But millions of unemployed persons and major underemployed industries are no rose in its buttonhole, no recommendation to new countries about to chart their course. They reduce America's potential for good work outside. An effective American foreign policy is unthinkable without a healthy—and therefore constantly expanding—economy.

The controversy about the desirable rate of American economic growth has been heated. Most authorities agree, however, on at least one proposition: if America's economy slips back, it will hurt Americans and the entire world. Professor Seymour E. Harris, chairman of the Department of Economics at Harvard University, favors "an annual growth rate of four to five per cent" instead of the 2 per cent in recent years "because," he wrote in the *New Leader* of May 30, 1960, "if the trend of the last few years continues, Soviet output by 1970 or 1975 will be close to ours."

Is the real issue not how much the United States should grow but how? Those who are satisfied with less expansion may fear that more could be the result only of government participation in economic affairs. If the alternative to this so-called socialism or new New Deal is stagnation, the choice is likely to be so-called socialism. In all countries the state steps in where private enterprise fails, so that the question of the rate of growth is really a challenge to private capitalism to make good or move over.

In this nuclear-jet-space age all major aspects of life and many minor ones hang together. Foreign policy reflects domestic politics and the domestic economy. The domestic economy shapes foreign aid. American foreign aid is, in part, cold warfare with Russia, in part, time-honored generosity, in part, the impulse to weave ties with other nations. For

Americans know in their bones, if they do not yet know with their brains, that to be only a nation alone is to prepare to die. To live is to grow in wealth and stature, and to grow in stature involves self-criticism, a keen awareness of others, and change.

Before sputnik, Soviet communism was something to abominate, underestimate, and ridicule. With the launching of the first Soviet space vehicle, Americans learned fear, and not so much fear of Russia as fear that the United States was no longer automatically, unalterably number one. This hurt. Americans began to examine themselves. Russian education, they said, was better than American education; the Soviet Union trained more scientists than the United States. They discovered other flaws and learned some humility. Hubris—the insolence of pride—vanished, took wing (and seems to have come to earth in the Kremlin).

But were teachers' salaries raised to attract more and better talent? How much does the United States spend on schools compared with alcohol? How much does the average or above-average family contribute through conversation, discussion, and good reading to raising the culture of its members and thus of the land? How much time and space do TV, radio, newspapers, and periodicals give to sex, sensation, murder, and trash, and how much to world affairs and domestic affairs? How much do individual Americans help—through aid to refugees, CARE parcels, UNICEF Christmas cards, inviting foreign visitors into their homes, exchange of letters and magazines—toward promoting sympathy among peoples? What special effort do Americans make to hear and understand the points of view of other countries and continents? Do even very intelligent Americans try to overcome their racial, religious, and national prejudices? All these things are relevant to America's foreign policy and to America's position in the world. "I am patriotic because I am human and humane," Mahatma Gandhi said. ". . . A patriot is so much less a patriot if he is a lukewarm humanitarian."

"My family is the world," Gandhi often repeated.

Every advanced country makes loans from other countries, loans of philosophy, science, music, literature, and so forth. The greater the international indebtedness the richer the lenders and the borrowers. John Milton wrote of "our greatest merchandize—truth." It should be high on all lists of exports and imports. John Stuart Mill said, "If all mankind minus one were of one opinion, and only one person were of the contrary opinion, mankind would be no more justified in silencing that one person, than he, if he had the power, would be justified in silencing mankind." Those who practiced this principle could preach it and the sermon would then penetrate iron, bamboo, indeed steel curtains.

Ideas are the true internationalists; they recognize no boundaries and cannot be stopped by them. Cultural cross-fertilization goes on all the time. Gandhi in South Africa and Count Leo Tolstoi in central Russia, though they had not met, shared their common views on nonviolence. Ralph Waldo Emerson read deeply in the Hindu Upanishads and infected Henry Thoreau, whose *Civil Disobedience* essay gave Gandhi the preferred name for his movement of peaceful resistance to evil. That closed one circle: India to America to India. Today there is another fruitful semicircle: American Negroes are putting Gandhi's civil disobedience into practice through their sit-in strikes in the southern states.

The most Rev. Denis Hurley, Roman Catholic archbishop of Durban, South Africa, told the London *Times* in an interview published August 25, 1960, that in his country "somehow the color bar had proved impervious to Christian charity." In the southern states the Rev. Martin Luther King and other avowed followers of Mahatma Gandhi borrowed

Gandhism to catalyze Christian charity. Gandhi was an eastern Christ functioning in complicated modern conditions and the civil disobedience techniques he evolved in South Africa and applied so effectively in India have struck root in America.

In a southern city a Negro college student sat on a stool at the lunch counter of a department store which had always refused to serve colored people. He was protesting against this discrimination by quietly sitting-in. From the stool next to him a white man blew cigar-smoke rings into the boy's face. Instead of punching the offender in the jaw, which would have been the "human" and "natural" reaction, the Negro "took" it, continued to sit and do nothing, thus displaying an active courage greater than that required for fighting with fists or weapons. This kind of nonretaliatory bravery, manifested in a thousand instances, marks the emergence of a new Negro who is defending his rights in person against odds. Disciplined self-respect makes others respect him. "I didn't think he had it in him," says the white man. The Negro is straightening his back so that nobody can ride on it. In the long run, and often in the short run, the Gandhian method is invincible. Already scores of southern restaurants and lunch counters are catering to Negroes seated next to whites. Perhaps the most creative by-product of this do-it-yourself emancipation is the co-operation of whites. Seeing Negro sit-in demonstrators jostled, insulted, threatened, sometimes mangled, white college and high school youths have joined the picket lines for a better America. India, Africa, and many Europeans read and admire and alter their opinions of U.S. democracy.

Gandhi to Virginia to Georgia to Texas forms a fertile semicircle. Someday India's sixty million untouchables may walk in the footsteps of the American Negro. Thus individuals weave threads of planetary understanding. Rendering medical therapy to the survivors of Hiroshima's bomb blast and of Hitler's murder camps is spiritual therapy. American physicians healing in Asian and African jungles are the fulfillment of peace on earth, good will to men. Foreign policy is made not only in the White House, State Department, and Senate. It is made in every heart, in every home, in every newspaper office, TV-radio station, local election, in every public action of the American people. Through invisible airwaves, but also through visible and audible ones, the wishes of the nation are communicated to the policy makers, and they listen or can be made to listen.

To sum up:

Along the NATO line from Norway to Turkey, American military power has prevented a third world war and will continue to deter. This contributed to the moderation of the political system inside Russia. In the future the United States should be firm without being provocative and conciliatory without retreating. There is a vast no man's land between indispensable containment and rigid hostility. The administration in Washington should explore it.

In Latin America, Africa, and Asia the United States, so rich in creative genius and other resources, should place a portion of this treasure at the disposal of the unhappy. It will thereby make them and itself happier.

The supreme goal of United States foreign policy should be a twentieth-century world in which all countries enjoy better living conditions and—what is no less important—better living, and therefore have an equal stake in freedom, justice, and tranquillity. Toward this end America should lead by example and help others in self-serving unselfishness.

# Index

# ABOUT THE AUTHOR

Louis Fischer was born and educated in Philadelphia. In 1921 he was sent to Berlin by the New York *Post* and spent most of the next twenty-five years on roving assignments in Europe and Asia.

He is a leading authority on Russia, where he spent many years, as well as on India and the Middle East. After covering the Spanish Civil War, he was in France when World War II broke out and he spent the first few months of the conflict practically commuting between London and Paris.

Since the war he has traveled throughout the world. He was in India in 1942, 1946, 1948, 1950, 1952, 1954, and 1958. In 1952 he made a round-the-world tour of nine months' duration that took him to Italy, Yugoslavia, West Germany, Pakistan, Burma, Siam, Indo-China, Hong Kong, the Philippines, Japan, and Alaska. He returned again to Germany during the last days of the Big Four conference. In 1955 he spent almost seven months abroad on extensive research in European countries. In 1956 he revisited Soviet Russia and Czechoslovakia; in 1957, Poland and Yugoslavia. In 1958 he spent three months in Indonesia and then two months in Holland. He went abroad again in 1959 and 1960. In each country that he has visited he has interviewed and watched virtually every important world leader at work. He was the house guest of Mahatma Gandhi in 1942 and 1946. He knew Roosevelt, Churchill, and Stalin. He has had several meetings with Tito and knows Nehru well.

Mr. Fischer is now at the Institute for Advanced Study in Princeton, New Jersey.